LEADING

ON

**THE GUIDE TO CREATING A
PURPOSE-DRIVEN CULTURE**

PURPOSE

NICK LEACH

R^ethink

First published in Great Britain 2020
by Rethink Press (www.rethinkpress.com)

Illustration, The Purpose Culture Journey, by Tatum Kenna
(www.tatumkenna.com).

Contents

Introduction

Once you have led a purpose-driven culture, you will be for ever on the hunt to find it again. It's infectious: you feel connected, part of a team that is changing the world, surpassing everyone's expectations in ways no one has ever thought of before. There is a magic and energy which become irresistible to everyone around you.

The problems that plague most organisations – such as margin control, talent retention, compliance issues and lack of innovation – don't exist in a purpose-driven organisation. Over the years I have created many high-performing teams and purpose-driven cultures. This book will provide you with the process and tools you need to create and lead with purpose.

THE PURPOSE CULTURE JOURNEY

MINDSET

POSSIBILITIES

TRUST

CREDIBILITY
RELIABILITY
INTIMACY
SELF-ORIENTATION

PURPOSE

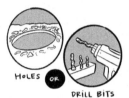

HOLES OR DRILL BITS

WHAT BUSINESS ARE YOU IN?

PURPOSE

WHAT CUSTOMERS ARE REALLY BUYING

UNIQUE QUALITIES OF YOUR BUSINESS

BUILD YOUR PURPOSE

TEAMS

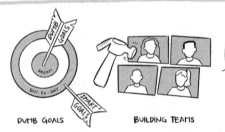

DUMB GOALS

DREAM
DAY-TO-DAY
SMART GOALS

DUMB GOALS

BUILDING TEAMS

UNLEASHING THE POWER OF TEAMS

SUSTAIN

THE POWER OF A JOURNEY

MEASURING SUCCESS

A purpose-driven culture has many benefits, which organisations often work on as individual topics without realising that the issues are related:

- Ambition

- Innovation

- Team engagement

- Speed and agility

- Financial performance

Frequently, purpose is seen in opposition to financial performance. People assume that you need to be tough and ruthless to make a profit. This is a myth: the difference in a purpose-driven culture is *how performance is achieved*. An organisation must be laser-focused on understanding and meeting the needs of its customers. Combined with ambition and innovation, this understanding produces solutions that customers are unaware that they want or need. These solutions will set you apart from competitors, and differentiate your organisation: you will become the leader in your field. Focus and passion will motivate and inspire you and your teams every day.

Three steps in this book will guide you to create your own purpose-led culture:

1. Mindset

2. Purpose

3. Unleashing the power of teams

Mindset

It all starts with mindset, as it is important that everyone's thinking is aligned and in the right frame of mind to create a purpose. First, you as the leader need to decide and be intentional about creating and living a purpose. As a leader, you are its evangelist: people need to see you, when they think of the purpose, and it's important that this is authentic and real. (Don't worry, by the time you finish the book you will be excited to move forward.)

Second, the next step is to help you and your teams see the possibilities in front of you. Most organisations tend to downward spiral a lot: 'Others are better', 'Others have more resources', 'It's impossible'. We need to change this type of thinking, so in Chapter 2 we will examine how to see the possibilities in front of you. The switch happens when you change from seeing all the issues to seeing opportunities. We need this before we can build a purpose statement, otherwise it may not be aspirational, and you won't be aiming high enough. When all you see are issues, everything seems impossible. When you see opportunities, you will aim for them.

Third, there is the topic of trust. It's a highly subjective issue: in Chapter 3 we will look at how trust can be analysed, so you can diagnose why there may be a trust issue in a relationship. This is powerful stuff, and transformational: it will bring trust to the centre of your organisation, ensuring that all relationships – both internal and external – have trust at their foundation. Trust is the glue of relationships, so it makes sense that it's also the glue in high-performing, purpose-driven organisations. Without trust in organisations there are hidden agendas, patch protection and teams focused on internal politics rather than customers.

By getting trust right and with a mindset of possibilities, we are ready to focus on purpose.

Purpose

Before creating a purpose statement, there is one more step: understanding the business you are in. While this may sound like a crazy question, let me clarify. The business you are in is determined by the *why* of your customers: for example, if your organisation makes drill bits, what are people buying? They are buying the hole, not a drill bit. In this case, your organisation isn't making drill bits, it's making holes. In the health industry, people don't buy pills, they buy wellness.

Understanding this is fundamental to building your purpose, as this must relate to what people are buying.

Once we're clear on the business we are in and what our customers really want, it's time to consider our purpose statement. This combines:

1. Your organisation's aspiration for your customers

2. What you want your organisation to be recognised for: the special and unique way you deliver to your customers

With the right purpose statement in place, to make it powerful we need to unleash the power of our teams to align our organisation to the purpose, and make it live every day in the DNA of our people. This book will provide you with the theory, tools and practical steps to make this happen.

Unleashing the power of teams

A purpose is only powerful when it's put into action: in organisations today, strategy and execution are delivered through teams. Understanding how to build and develop high-performing teams ensures that your purpose is executed through innovative and inspirational customer solutions.

High-performing teams have infectious drive and energy. They create and execute unique strategies that see them outperform competitors. In these teams, camaraderie drives a sense a loyalty and belonging, for which we all strive.

The simple model presented in this book will help you create the qualities needed to build high-performing teams. In the Appendix there is also a workshop guide to help you put it into practice. The high-performing team model will ensure that your organisation's purpose lives every day in its execution, and stands out both from the crowd and your competitors. This becomes your own style, which resonates with customers and the people you serve.

Now we have the right mindset, a powerful purpose statement and high-performing teams delivering strategies, with execution aligned to the purpose, there is only one topic left to discuss: how do we sustain momentum?

The key to continued performance and forward motion is for leaders to recognise that the organisation is on a continuous journey.

Organisations on a journey

Setting your business on a journey is not difficult, but it does make a world of difference to organisational performance and team mindset. Being on a journey means that your organisation is constantly progressing to achieve its purpose. Change is a recognised, perpetual part of the organisation's DNA. This ensures that even long-term team members do not become stuck in their ways, and that everyone is open to change.

When change is constant and anticipated, people are open to new ideas and finding new ways to do things. You become the leader of change, not the victim of it.

To recognise the journey, key performance indicators (KPIs) are designed to measure the progress to achieving something, rather than a binary achieve/ fail goal such as a financial KPI. KPIs recognise the pathway, helping teams understand what has been accomplished, and what is left to do, keeping people constantly thinking and looking ahead.

With the right mindset, a great purpose powered by high-performing teams who are on a journey builds a great, purpose-led culture.

About me

Even as a child, I was fascinated by and interested in business – I wanted to be an entrepreneur. I couldn't wait to leave school and get stuck in, as I come from a family which has run its own businesses. I studied accounting part-time, as I knew this would be a great and necessary skill: to understand a profit and loss and balance sheet and recognise the importance of cashflow, and to be able to forecast with a degree of accuracy.

While I worked at an accounting firm, I set up an office night-cleaning business, Action Cleaning Services. A few years later, I moved into the car business, like my uncle, working for a Toyota dealer in Wellington, New Zealand, as the administration manager. In my early twenties I had been fortunate enough to attend a business summit where Jason Jennings, the American bestselling business author, shared with us the nine qualities of the most successful companies in the world. The first was: 'The most successful businesses in the world have a cause.' The word 'cause' puts purpose into action – a cause is something people fight for, just as you want them to fight for your organisation and its purpose.

When I came back from this conference, I set about working with the leaders of the car dealership to introduce a cause. With hindsight, I now realise I made the mistake that most organisations make: we presented the cause, put it on our logo – and that was it. We didn't work at making it part of everything we did. We missed the vital link, from purpose to strategy to execution.

It wasn't until later in my career, as country manager of a pharmaceutical company in New Zealand, that I had the opportunity to create a purpose-led culture. This wasn't common in pharma; everything was scientific and logical. Historically, it was the science and the patent which drove the return. People were focused on financial planning; no one really cared about the strategy – ironic, considering that the numbers are the result of strategy.

I knew that my team were inspired by what we did, but they were not unified in their focus. Everyone had their own way of saying the same thing: they were inspired by the fact we helped people; but without a purpose, this was a personal motivator which was not part of day-to-day decision making. Putting a purpose in place, and being intentional and bold in decision making, ensured that our purpose was our guide. This was powerful, as all the team's personal motivations became that of the organisation: true alignment, our North Star.

It was not until two to three years later that I recognised the need to improve teamwork to drive better performance. Once introduced to the model in this book, it was like I had found the answer to the universe! It made all the difference, driving our purpose and performance more than I could ever have imagined.

I still get comments today about the legacy I left behind in that organisation, how people found it inspirational. It was the purpose that sparked inspiration, and people found it so only because everyone in the organisation believed in the 'Unstoppable Drive to Restore People's Lives'. More importantly, the team could see that we were making decisions based on this – we lived the purpose every day. This purpose-driven culture achieved the highest turnover and growth in the industry for five consecutive years: clear proof that purpose can drive performance.

Summary

In this book, my promise to you is that we will cover all the ingredients you need to create a purpose-led culture. If you follow through on this checklist, you will achieve it and feel more rewarded than ever in your role:

1. Drive a mindset of possibilities

2. Understand and implement trust throughout your organisation

3. Understand the business you are in, and what your customers are buying

4. Build a compelling purpose with your leadership team

5. Unleash the power of teams to achieve the DUMB goals

6. Set your organisation on a journey to demonstrate and live the purpose

7. Measure your progress to the purpose

With these in place, your organisation will indeed be changing the world and making it a better place for everyone.

Let's get going!

1
Why Purpose?

If we look at the beginning of all great companies, there has always been a passionate person there, with a vision to change the world in some way. Purpose was the genesis of this creation. Over time, and as organisations get bigger, purpose becomes lost, replaced by policies, procedures, meetings and quarterly targets.

Bringing purpose back to the centre of the organisation reconnects everyone to what made it successful in the first place. Purpose inspires everyone who has contact with your organisation. Inspiration leads to ambition, which then drives innovation and unique strategies, which ultimately leads to superior performance.

Without purpose, what is the reason for your organisation's existence? Why do your people come to work every day? And why do they work for you? It's surprising just how many organisations can't answer these questions. Without purpose, are your people just working for a pay cheque, happy to exist with more interests outside of work? In the absence of passion and ambition, your teams are simply waiting for something better to come along.

Creating a purpose-driven culture is good for everyone: it's what makes humanity great, a vision to believe in something bigger than ourselves. Life's too short – we need our people to jump out of bed every morning, excited about the day ahead!

Some organisations recognise the importance of having a purpose. They commission management consultants, like McKinsey & Company, to create one, and launch it throughout the organisation. Job done, right? Wrong. In reality it has no impact, merely 'words on a wall'. The issue is not whether you do or don't have a purpose statement; it's about having one that influences people every day, and is part of your organisation's DNA.

This is a trap that so many fall into: they have a purpose statement, ticking the boxes. But this is just the beginning, because it's not what we say that matters, it's what we do. These organisations miss the link from purpose to strategy to execution. The vital step to strategy is how we put purpose into action.

Having an outside consultant providing you with the purpose is a flawed approach. First, it shows everyone that it obviously isn't important enough for the senior leaders to do it; or worse still, that they don't have the skill. To make that link, senior leaders must be involved in creating the purpose, and truly believe that the organisation can live and progress to achieving it. In a PwC survey of business leaders, 79% recognised that having a purpose beyond profit is key to their future success, while 68% shared that the purpose is not used in leadership or any decision making.[1]

To show how powerful purpose can be, let's look at a great example. The New Zealand All Blacks, the most successful rugby team in the history of the world, have a purpose statement which ensures everyone who puts on the national jersey takes responsibility to be their best.

WHAT WILL BE YOUR COMPANY LEGACY?

The New Zealand All Blacks are known throughout the world for their teamwork and fierce passion for the game of rugby. Each member is a role model for the country's children and this responsibility pushes them to aim higher and ensure they only improve the image and

---

1   'Putting Purpose to Work: A study of purpose in the workplace', PwC, 2016, www.pwc.com/us/en/purpose-workplace-study.html

legacy of the team. This is perfectly embodied in their long-held saying: 'Leave the jersey in a better place'.

'Better people make better All Blacks – but they also make better doctors and lawyers, bankers and businessmen, fathers, brothers and friends.'[2]

When a player puts on the All Blacks jersey, they have a sense of pride beyond any other team. This can be the same for your organisation: working for it will be different to working for anyone else in your industry.

I don't know about you, but this speaks to everyone in a way that inspires, builds trust and speaks to the soul and passion of the team.

There are several benefits of a purpose-driven culture.

Employee engagement

Having a purpose-driven culture is going to be the key to future success of any organisation. In the same PwC research mentioned earlier, millennials are 5.3 times more likely to stay at a company when they believe in what it's doing. Currently, 33% of people feel engaged and believe their organisation is trying to

2   J Kerr, 'The All Blacks Guide to being successful', *The Telegraph*, 14 November 2013, www.telegraph.co.uk/men/active/10427619/The-All-Blacks-guide-to-being-successful-off-the-field.html

achieve its purpose.[3] We all know that with meaning and purpose in our life, we feel significantly happier than if we are just existing. Because we spend so much of our time working, it makes sense to get fulfilment from our work. The beauty of a purpose-driven culture is that it gives meaning to an organisation, and is something everyone can be proud of.

So many organisations work on employee engagement by improving the cafeteria and putting on free lunches. They miss the point, failing to recognise that employee engagement is actually the result of how fulfilled they feel at work, whether they think they're making a positive difference in the world.

Purpose keeps you honest

Living your purpose statement means that when you're developing strategies, they must show the company purpose – which sometimes can seem to go against conventional thinking. This can be a powerful benefit.

When I worked in pharma, we were launching a new product: a cure for people living with a terrible disease. It was a revolutionary product with an expensive price tag. The wisdom at the

---

3   'Putting Purpose to Work: A study of purpose in the workplace', PwC, 2016 www.pwc.com/us/en/purpose-workplace-study.html

time was to limit access to the people who most needed it – only the very sick, which would help the health systems manage the budget.

At the time, our purpose statement said that we put the patient at the centre of everything we do. For me and my team, limiting access to the cure to only the very sick did not align with our purpose, so it drove us to find another way.

We brainstormed different ideas and came up with a novel and highly unconventional funding model, which many thought crazy at the time. But by thinking differently, driven by our purpose, it made us strive to come up with a strategy which won us the business!

It turned out to be extremely successful. The government payer loved the idea, as they were about to give the cure to all, and could at the same time manage the budget impact.

At the time, a competitor had a similar product which, we soon came to realise, had benefits over our product. They were also in discussions with the payer, proposing a traditional funding arrangement, limiting access only to the sickest patients. Our unique model was much more attractive to our payer, and outweighed their product's superiority.

> We were successful because we challenged our-
> selves to think differently and come up with an
> innovative solution, driven by a team staying
> honest to the purpose.

This is a fundamental rule of purpose-driven organisations: always stay true to your purpose. The minute your purpose statement becomes optional, the impact is lost – more importantly, trust in the leadership is lost, as the leaders say one thing and do another. This is where leaders must be ruthless: anything that challenges your purpose must be dealt with in the same way that you would fight anyone who threatens someone you care about.

Staying true to your cause will make you think differently, and drive you to be more innovative in your approach.

Reputation

It takes 20 years to build a reputation and five minutes to ruin it. If you think about that, you'll do things differently.
    — Warren Buffett[4]

---

4   Cited in B Tuttle, 'Warren Buffett's boring, brilliant wisdom', *Time*, 1 March 2010, https://business.time.com/2010/03/01/warren-buffetts-boring-brilliant-wisdom

In most companies, this quote is used like a weapon by compliance and legal teams: 'You'd better listen to me – I'm saving your reputation, and you know the cost of getting it wrong!' It scares people into doing nothing, or accepting whatever legal or compliance tells them.

Business is always grey

The challenge for many businesses is that most of their activities are not black or white, compliant or non-compliant: they live somewhere in the grey area. Thousands of meetings and watered-down initiatives are caused by not having a framework to understand how to navigate that grey area.

This is the power of a purpose-driven culture: creating a framework to consider grey-area initiatives. It comes down to intention: does this move us closer to achieving the purpose, or not? This becomes even more important when your organisation is leading the way and doing things first and differently to others.

It's time to change how your organisation considers reputation. Reputation is not gained or lost on one initiative or executing one idea, it's about an organisation's ethos and how well it lives up to its purpose. If your organisation demonstrates its actions and intention, lives its purpose and executes to it, your reputation will be solid, respected and trusted – especially by its stakeholders – as the organisation is trying to do the right thing.

Even if something goes awry – for example, a bad hire who does something wrong and you have to take corrective action – this shouldn't destroy your reputation, especially if you can show you are actively addressing it. People can clearly see what has happened. With a strong bond of trust, it's likely that your stakeholders may even come out to defend you! The above quote only needs weaponising in organisations which are solely profit-focused – they need to make sure their people operate inside the rules, to avoid being sued.

You will see a great example in Chapter 5 that in purpose-driven cultures, compliance is different. It becomes an enabler, helping your teams to navigate grey areas and find ways to execute safely to be successful.

Time to decide

By the time you have read this book, I'm sure I will have convinced you to lead a purpose-driven culture. It rests with you to decide. You need courage to follow through and live it every day, call it out when people are making bad decisions. Sometimes, it will be saying 'No' to a commercial return.

Once you have decided, know this: your teams will test you before they are on board – they want proof that you mean what you say. Testing you against commercial gain will be the greatest test. Don't worry: the loss will be far outweighed by future gain.

I can still remember the day I decided I wanted to change the way I was leading the organisation, and what it stood for. At the time, I didn't know that I wanted to create a purpose-led culture. I had a fantastic team, and I knew they didn't come to work just for the money or the purpose of the larger multinational company. Everyone had different reasons, but all had a link to helping people, so I set about to change it. I also knew I wanted to differentiate who we were from the market, as we acted differently to everyone else.

At the time, we were looking for an advertising agency to help us with branding and marketing our key products. We had agencies come and pitch for the business. One in particular stood out for me because of one guy: when he walked in, there was no hype, he looked me in the eye and said 'Hi'.

Through the pitch, others would talk about things. I responded by talking about how as a team we passionately cared for the patients we were serving. Then this person leaned into the table, looked me in the eye and said:

'Yeah – it's about the people, and the why.'

Instantly, in my mind, they were hired.

We then set about our purpose workshop. What was important to me at the time was that it had to be our truth, not a slogan – it had to mean something to everyone who worked in our organisation. The result was: 'An Unstoppable Drive to Restore People's Lives'. I couldn't imagine at that moment how much this would change my life; I was just excited to go to work and change the world.

We made a significant difference in the way we worked, which translated into success. Within five years, this purpose-driven culture created the largest pharma company in the country: something no one else has been able to achieve.

Like my example, if you want to do this, you have to lead and make it your number one priority – because without your leadership and belief, it will not work. You can bring in external agencies to help you build your purpose statement, but you can't delegate it to them. You will only be passionate about something you create. You also need to work on this with your senior leaders: they must have a sense of ownership too.

Later in Chapter 5, we will discuss building your purpose statement, but for now I just want to stress the need to decide and commit.

The courage to follow through

It will take courage to follow through on creating a purpose-driven culture. It will take time for people to understand that this is not just another 'here today, gone tomorrow' campaign. Once you make this change, your organisation will be transformed, people will be excited to come to work again, and your strategies and execution will become more exciting and innovative.

Courage is important right from the beginning: all your decisions from this point onwards must be aligned. An organisation that picks and chooses when to align will not achieve a purpose-driven culture; instead, what you will have is teams of people who don't trust their senior leaders' decision making.

Are you ready to begin the journey? I promise that it will be just as exciting as the destination, a rewarding process that will drive your passion and change your life. You'll never want to go back.

When I set to work building a purpose-led culture, I knew my regional boss would not necessarily buy into my idea. Obviously if they thought purpose was important, they would be doing it right. I had to have the courage to move forward and risk being different to my boss.

It totally paid off in the end. I took courage from the words of Theodore Roosevelt's 'Citizenship in the Republic' speech which he gave at the Sorbonne, Paris, in 1910: 'It is not the critic who counts... The credit belongs to the man who is actually in the arena... who strives valiantly... who spends himself for a worthy cause'.[5]

Be the person in the arena, leading a company to change the world. Take pride in your work and your people. Together you can achieve greatness!

The line 'Culture eats strategy for breakfast'[6] pops up on LinkedIn about every fortnight but it's a terrible

5   'Quotations from the speeches and other works of Theodore Roosevelt' Theodore Roosevelt Association, www.theodoreroosevelt.org/content.aspx?page_id=22&club_id=991271&module_id=339333
6   This quote is sometimes, but probably mistakenly, attributed to Peter Drucker.

saying – it shouldn't be one or the other. In fact, you can't have one without the other.

Without a great strategy you will not build a great culture, and without a great culture, it will be extremely difficult to have a good strategy. The link from purpose and strategy to execution is key, as it helps propel your purpose-driven culture.

Generally, all organisations have the basics in place, respect their people, create a safe environment, etc. These are not game changers, they're expectations. Once these are in place, again, inspiring your people with the reason why they come to work will be the game changer for your culture.

Inspirational leadership

Great leaders don't set out to be a leader... they set out to make a difference. It's never about the role – always about the goal.
— Warren Bennis[7]

I love this quote, as it's so true. I have often been called an inspirational leader, but there is nothing inspirational about me. What people found inspirational was the purpose of the business I became the evangelist

---

7   Cited in R Ashgar, 'Why real leaders don't set out to become leaders', *Forbes*, 16 June 2014, www.forbes.com/sites/robasghar/2014/06/16/why-real-leaders-dont-set-out-to-become-leaders/#5096e1f91e08

for: people are inspired by your drive to see the organisation achieve its noble goals. By doing so, you are enabling others to be their best, constantly challenged by trying new things and growing.

This is the key to great leadership: get the purpose right, then drive it.

Proof of this is Steve Jobs. He was said to be terrible to work for, but he was relentless in his pursuit of what he believed was right for consumers.[8] He would often make decisions which were best for customers rather than for Apple, but in turn he created one of the most successful organisations of all time. He was inspirational because he believed in thinking differently, and didn't stop until he brought the best products to market.

If you want to be an inspirational leader, read on.

To close this chapter and show the power of purpose, consider your organisation. Which side are you on currently?

---

8   L Butcher, cited in J Taylor, 'Zen and the art of computing,' *The New York Times*, 25 October 1987, www.nytimes.com/1987/10/25/books/books-and-business-zen-and-the-art-of-computing.html

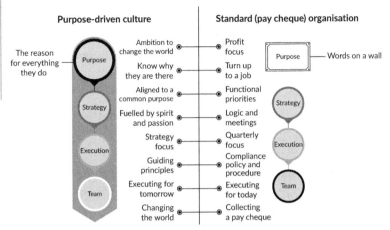

Working for purpose vs pay cheque

2

Possibilities

Before we even begin to discuss purpose, it is important to work on mindset and understand the power of possibilities. By the end of this chapter you will see the world differently.

Have you ever noticed how it's easier to believe the negative things that people say, rather than the positives? And if someone says something positive, they must want something, right? In the world today we seem to be more critical, looking for what's wrong rather than seeing what's right. (If you want to talk to people who are always positive, speak to a child!)

The result is that businesses have been set up with legal and compliance to counsel on the worst-case scenario, which always seems easier to believe than the power of a potential new opportunity. The opportunity is the unknown, but compliance and legal are certain on the jail time!

To become a purpose-driven culture, we need to change this.

Look for opportunities

We need to flip the script and look for the possibilities around us. *The Art of Possibilities* by Ben Zander has been a key to my own success.[9] Not positive thinking or just saying something is good when it isn't; rather, looking for opportunities in everything. A story within the book tells of a couple of shoe salesmen visiting Africa in the 1900s. Upon arrival they observed that no one wore shoes. When they sent telegrams back to the office, the first commented that the situation was hopeless as they don't wear shoes; the second wrote of a 'glorious opportunity' because they don't have any shoes yet!.

As leaders, the words we use matter: we have a choice of 'Glorious opportunity', or 'Situation hopeless'. The two shoe salespeople had the same conditions, the market was the same, but the words they used dramatically changed the outcome. One company is

9   B Zander, *The Art of Possibility: Practices in Leadership, Relationship and Passion* (Penguin, 2006)

looking at how to sell shoes in Africa, and the other has given up as the situation is seen as a non-starter.

Can you imagine the difference in these two companies' results? One organisation with the power of possibilities will be successful in selling shoes in Africa. The other will fall into the downward spiral and sell none.

Glorious opportunity	Situation hopeless
How can we?	It can't be done.
Wow, that's exciting!	That seems risky.
It's not what we wanted, so what did we learn?	This is terrible.
Let's try this!	That won't work.

In a culture of possibilities, you'll be amazed at the opportunities coming your way that are missed by your competitors. This mindset has to start at the top, with senior leaders. A company living the art of possibilities is a lot more fun to work in too: no doom and gloom; instead, scope, excitement and energy.

What sort of company would you rather work for?

Changing your organisation to see possibilities will take some time, but it starts with your ability to master the art of recognising them. If you are coming from a predominately profit-driven organisation, it is important to remember that your team default is to downward spiral: to view everything your organisation does as a risk, rather than an opportunity. Right now, your people are likely to be frustrated, as every idea becomes so diluted by compliance and legal that there is almost no point in trying anymore. Eventually they just stop trying and only do what needs to be done and coast for their pay.

Putting your purpose at the centre of your business and using it as a judgement for initiatives will help your teams begin to see things in a better way than the worst-case scenario. It will take time and your leadership to stop them from heading for the downward spiral.

> When I was leading a New Zealand organisation, once we had established the 'Unstoppable Drive to Restore People's Lives', I would show in meetings on how to judge initiatives against it.
>
> Over time, what I found was that our teams came up with different ideas and initiatives which the 'standard rules' were not designed to cover. This is when you know you are thought leaders. In these circumstances it becomes easier to navigate if your teams are purpose-driven and live in a world of possibilities. This is magic: without the purpose as a reference, few initiatives would have been approved.

The power of possibilities is most important in the face of bad news, people will look to you and watch how you respond. If you spiral downwards into the negative, so will they. This isn't easy at first – sometimes you'll feel you want to – but you can't. Instead, you could say: 'This is unfortunate and not what we want, but what can we learn from it – how does this now affect our plans?'

This is a far more measured approach, and it's in these circumstances that our focus on possibilities includes watching the words we use, as discussed previously.

I have also experienced the situation when initially a market change was thought to be bad, but with possibilities it became an opportunity. I took the reins and asked the necessary questions to identify the learning and response required.

The team took this focus on board and worked out how to make the situation benefit us. It was genius! If we had given up, we would have completely missed the change we needed to make.

After this, people would come up and say: 'You were so lucky.' But luck had nothing to do with it.

You have to create your own luck. You have to be aware of the opportunities around you and take advantage of them.
— Bruce Lee[10]

Logic versus emotion

The essential difference between emotion and reason is that emotion leads to action, while reason leads to conclusions.
— Donald Calne[11]

Reason and logic are fantastic, but tell me any great achievement in the world which came from logic and reason? It always starts with emotion. Emotion is what drives us. Even for scientists, whom you would consider extremely logical people, it's their passion which leads them to action. They come up with logical conclusions from experiments, but passion is what gets them excited to experiment in the first place.

A business full of logic and no passion will not change the world, simply focused on following trend lines, data analysis and meetings. You can find logical reasons for almost anything, but they don't make it necessary.

10   B Lee, L Lee and T Bleecker, *The Bruce Lee Story* (Black Belt Communications, 1989), p116
11   D Calne, *Within Reason: Rationality and Human Behavior* (Vintage, 2000)

One example of this is in many large multinationals, there has been a massive increase in legal documentation required of suppliers so that the company is protected from the worst-case scenario; but the challenge is that this comes at a cost of time and resources to cover what, in many cases, are low-risk transactions. Resource that could be better spent supporting the purpose.

Possibilities brings spirit to your organisation. With your new, purpose-driven culture there will be less bad news to worry about, as your organisation now has a reason to exist other than to make money. Emotion is the counterbalance to logic. And logic, while important, doesn't lead to achieving big dreams. Big dreams come from our emotional side, our passion. The power of humanity is our ability to balance logic and emotion, but the challenge in most organisations is that the emotion and passion are missing. Possibilities harness our emotions and bring them back into our organisations. In a world of seeing opportunities, it is easier to think big and change the game – it becomes natural.

Possibilities also lead to big goals, and big goals are important. Many people fear setting them as, ultimately, they will have to meet them and there is a fear of failure. A big goal is important: without it your teams have no target to aim for, and aren't considering how to achieve it.

We will cover this more in 'DUMB goals' (see Chapter 6), but for now, let's look at why big goals matter.

When President John F. Kennedy said, 'We choose to go to the Moon', his speech set US space scientists on a path. The next morning, NASA scientists woke up and asked the question: how? Without the goal, it would never have happened. Imagine your organisation has a series of big goals, and your teams are aligned to focus on achieving them. Logic says we must have SMART goals, but possibilities allow us to focus on 'DUMB' goals.

Stay motivated

In my experience with a purpose-driven culture, I would receive compliments from people about myself, my team or working with our organisation. One of the ways I found helpful to stay focused on possibilities was to print the compliments out and keep them on file.

Then, when the going got tough, I would pull them out and read them. They gave me the courage to continue.

One thing you must do from now on is to remember the compliments and forget the insults. When your thoughts become possibilities, imagine your destiny!

Watch your thoughts, they become words;
watch your words, they become actions;
watch your actions, they become habits;
watch your habits, they become character;
watch your character, for it becomes your destiny.
— Frank Outlaw[12]

This quote is so powerful, it shows how we can be conditioned to the negative instead of the positive. There is no success to protect you from the downward spiral. We have already seen the difference between an organisation looking for opportunities, versus an organisation looking for issues.

I have seen many organisations where it seems they have meetings just to work out why they shouldn't do something, as opposed to why they should. These organisations' results will be very different. The purpose-driven organisation comes up with initiatives and creative solutions for customers, while its competitors try to copy. They will be wondering how you came up with such innovative solutions!

Make your own luck

Possibilities attract luck. People want to help people who are trying to do something exciting and for the benefit of others.

12 Cited in 'What they're saying', *San Antonio Light*, 18 May 1977

At one pharma company where I worked, we had a major goal to secure funding for our cure. We decided we needed to talk with the Government about this and the opportunity it provided to effectively eradicate a disease from the country.

We needed to understand how to work with government better, so we brought in a consultant to advise us. We shared with them our ambition and challenges. About a month into this project, the consultant highlighted an opportunity to appear before the Government Health Select Committee and raise the profile of the disease.

We seized the opportunity with open arms and immediately began discussions with clinicians – the best people to present to the Government. The key person was also the adviser to the government reimbursement agency, and firmly loyal to our main competitor. We engaged him, and he was one of the keynote speakers.

This was a game changer! Through working with our team and getting the presentation done, his view of our organisation changed – in fact, he couldn't believe the work we were doing to shape the environment for people living with a terrible disease.

In Chapter 3 we will see how this builds a foundation of trust between key stakeholders and organisations – but for now, this is a great example of making your own luck. Without the ambition and need to engage with the government consultant, we would never have known about the opportunity. Moreover, we would never have engaged our competitor's key opinion leader, who now had a completely different perspective on our organisation.

In an organisation busy working on the day-to-day, opportunities like this never just happen. You have to be in a position to see the possibilities, with the ambition to be out there.

Just remember the shoe salesperson story: it will keep you focused on making sure you are finding the opportunities in front of you.

Summary

1. It's important to break out of negative worst-case scenarios.

2. Recognise the downward spiral, 'Situation hopeless' or 'Glorious opportunity'. The words you use matter.

3. Recognise the power of emotion and passion. These qualities lead to action and execution.

4. Possibilities create ambition and big goals, which in turn drive innovation.

5. When you see the world through possibilities, you will attract your own luck.

3
Trust

Trust is the new currency of our interdependent, collaborative world.
— Stephen Covey[13]

Nothing happens without trust. A high level of trust is a key quality of a purpose-driven culture. This chapter will explain why, introduce you to a great model to unpack the notion of trust, and help you understand how to improve it in any given situation.

Trust is the foundation of any relationship, whether personally or professionally. Within high-performing organisations, trust is at the centre: people who don't trust each other will not work together. Trust

---

13 www.speedoftrust.com

also helps your organisation build better and stronger relationships with your customers, also moving them from transactional to more of a business partnership.

Trust is an emotive topic: to say you don't trust someone will have people coming out fighting; it brings out negative passion. An easy way to determine lack of trust is when faced with a challenging situation: are people able to have the discussion, or does it become emotional? Without trust, people take challenges personally, rather than understanding them from an organisational perspective.

When you search online, there are hundreds of articles about the importance of trust. This topic is so popular as trust isn't tangible: many people have different ideas and ways that they think help build trust. Like most intangible qualities, trust is the result of many inputs – so to improve it, you need to understand what is driving the gap. Rather than saying to someone, 'I want to work on building better trust with you', put more effort into the relationship.

The Trust Equation

In this chapter, the Trust Equation unpacks the concept, helping you identify the areas you may need to work on to improve trustworthiness.

The Trust Equation, developed by David Maister in *The Trusted Advisor*, is a helpful tool to use for this purpose.[14]

In much of this book we discuss the importance of passion and bringing emotion back into the business; but with trust, we want to do the opposite – to think of it logically and rationally. The beauty of the Trust Equation is that it removes emotion and helps us think in a more rational way.

I was introduced to the Trust Equation a few years back in an organisational culture workshop. I was seriously impressed that it worked, how it was possible to unpack trust into components.

When you break the equation down, you can understand what is driving trust issues, which you can then work on and resolve. Since learning the equation, it has helped me find the answer in every situation where I have had an issue with trust. Once you understand trust, it becomes much easier to build.

Using the Trust Equation throughout your organisation will ensure you build strong relationships with your team, stakeholders, customers and suppliers.

---

14   D Maister, R Galford and C Green, *The Trusted Advisor* (Simon & Schuster, 2002)

$$\text{Trust} = \frac{\text{Credibility} + \text{Reliability} + \text{Intimacy}}{\text{Self-orientation}}$$

The Trust Equation[15]

Credibility

This is a person's experience and training in a given field. For example, a doctor has credibility from their years of experience and the medical degrees they hold.

Reliability

• Do you follow through on what you say?

• Can you be counted on to deliver?

I am sure right now someone will come to mind whom you cannot rely on to do so – and because of this, you don't really trust them.

Intimacy

• Can I speak with you in confidence?

• Can I rely on you to keep things confidential?

15   D Maister, R Galford and C Green, *The Trusted Advisor* (Simon & Schuster, 2002)

- With bad news, can I trust that you won't lose your temper?

- Do I feel OK to ask you something which makes me vulnerable?

I worked for a leader who would fly off the handle and become aggressive with people when he didn't agree, but at other times he was an inspirational leader.

That inspiration completely evaporated, as no one could trust him to stay calm: they were walking on eggshells all the time. It didn't matter whether it was an occasional rant or not; the potential was always there for him to lose his cool. In this case, the potential to fly off the handle reduced his intimacy so much that no one could trust him.

These first three qualities in the equation are common ones that most people intuitively work on in their relationships. What may not be as clear is what's below the line: self-orientation.

Self-orientation

This is the biggie: the denominator that can quickly counter all the hard work being done above the line.

Self-orientation relates to how much of the agenda is about *you*; for this value you need to score low. Think about whether a person is asking themselves:

- Is it all about what *I* want?

- Are there benefits to *me* in understanding the other person's agenda and working together to accomplish their goals?

You may know this type of person: it's always about them and what they want, and you may not feel a strong bond of trust when dealing with them.

Regardless of your 'scores' above the line, the dominator, self-orientation, plays a pivotal role in building trust. In my experience, when trust is an issue in business, it's generally high self-orientation that's to blame.

- As a leader, what do you know about the other person and what they want to accomplish?

- Do you have any interest in understanding what they would like to achieve?

Many organisations are so focused on their internal goals and driving their own agenda that they forget to even consider what their customers want.

- Do you think your customers trust you?

- Would you trust an organisation that is solely interested in its own agenda?

In this type of organisation, the customer relationships will be transactional and because it suits them. No one is loyal.

It amazes me how many people miss the importance of trust in, and respect for, their customers. I have heard presentations where people talk about 'leveraging customers'. The definition of 'leverage' is to apply pressure to get what you want: this is the opposite of self-orientation! When the people in your organisation begin to understand the equation and apply it, they will soon realise that you would never use 'leverage' in this context.

The impact of trust

Now that we understand trust and the role it plays, consider how this impacts different parts of your organisation. In a lot of industries, representative incentives are in direct opposition to building trust. If the person in front of you effectively makes their salary only by you buying from them, there is a clear self-orientation that limits their ability to build a long-term, trusting relationship with their customers. At best, the relationship will be a transactional one.

Some in the pharmaceutical industry argue that without incentives, people would not be motivated to do their jobs. I've always found this a silly argument. If you take 40% of someone's expected salary and use it as a carrot, you're forcing their motivation to be connected to money – it's the lowest common denominator. Would you hire someone whose only motivation was money?

Take a minute to think about your organisation. Do you have policies or incentives that are counterproductive to building trust?

Build trust through your organisation

To build strong relationships with customers, colleagues and suppliers that last the test of time, you must share common goals that you are all actively working on achieving. This means alignment in self-orientation: you are working together to achieve the same result. This is a far better position for everyone. Transactional selling works in the short term, and it is likely the product is selling itself.

The first job of a leader – at work or at home – is to inspire trust. It's to bring out the best in people by entrusting them with meaningful stewardships, and to

create an environment in which high-trust interaction inspires creativity and possibility.
— Stephen Covey[16]

Another great outcome of building trust throughout your organisation is that it supports the culture and ability for people to be confident to say what they think. With a foundation in place, the culture becomes more open, so people feel comfortable to challenge when they have an alternative idea or position.

We can all remember a time when we knew a strategy was wrong, but we didn't feel we could say anything. In a purpose-driven organisation where people trust each other, you will find people will be comfortable to call it out – there is a level of transparency and no hidden agendas.

According to Stephen Covey's *The Speed of Trust*, getting rid of hidden agendas, and having greater transparency, increases your organisational trust factor.[17] People are motivated, communication is clear and when there are issues, they are highlighted and resolved. It's truly transformational.

Teach everyone the Trust Equation: make it part of your organisation's DNA, and trust will live at its

---

16 S Covey, *The Speed of Trust: The One Thing that Changes Everything* (Simon & Schuster, 2008), p333
17 S Covey, *The Speed of Trust*

centre. You will build a company with a best-in-class, leading reputation, and it will be difficult for any competitor to compete. Best of all, they won't understand why your organisation is succeeding. Understanding this will have your teams building trusting relationships with your customers, and mutual goals.

The topic of the next chapter is all about self-orientation, understanding from your customers' perspective what are they buying. This will be used to help build your organisation's purpose: trust is one of the main reasons for doing this. If we want to align to our customers' agenda, we need to understand what they ultimately want. This ensures that your purpose is aligned to your customers' real needs, and to your organisation's agenda.

With this valuable insight, trust will become instinctive in your daily operating rhythm, making it more natural to build better relationships. You'll take the time to understand others, and always be looking for mutual alignment.

Summary

1. Trust is the bedrock of all relationships. It needs to live at the centre of your organisation.

2. Learn the Trust Equation, and ensure that everyone in your organisation understands it.

3. Self-orientation is often the biggest derailer of trust. Agenda alignment with customers generates both a foundation of trust and lasting relationships to stand the test of time.

4. A foundation of trust drives a culture of transparency, removing hidden agendas.

4
What Business Are You In?

Understanding the business you are in is such a simple concept. When you get it right, it can transform both your thinking and the strategies that you and your team create.

In sales, this is often called 'solution selling': when people buy a drill bit, what they want is the hole it creates. Power comes not just from applying this concept in sales, but across your entire organisation. Imagine you're a drill bit manufacturer: with your teams focused on delivering holes, you will soon find your strategies and product innovations changing to focus on producing the best holes.

In the pharma industry, I quickly learned that a lot of mistrust between the government payer and suppliers related to reliability and self-orientation in the Trust Equation. The big disconnect was that the payer wanted to buy 'wellness', and the pharma companies were supplying drugs. This impacted reliability, as the payer never actually knew the benefit of what they were buying: having lost that, both parties focused instead on driving their own separate agendas.

Once I understood this disconnect, we made wellness the heart of our purpose, restoring lives. We believed that wellness was the government payer's goal, and restoring life was the patient's goal. This significantly impacted our responsibility and strategies, as it meant we needed to work closer with a broader stakeholder group to ensure we delivered wellness, not just a drug.

Moreover, we often had to put aside our agenda with stakeholders to build and develop a trusting relationship. We were invited to many meetings that other pharma companies weren't able to attend, because we were a trusted partner with an aligned goal: making people well.

We brought valuable insight to the table, so we could actively contribute.

This changed everything. Opportunities came to us as we were trusted partners, not just a drug supplier. This meant that many initiatives we funded in the interest of patients had no real financial return for our organisation. If accountants were to measure return on investment, it would look like a fail. But it was precisely these initiatives which always returned so much more in the long run than financial gain: some were totally inspiring, both for our stakeholders and our teams. This forged bonds which would last a lifetime.

Our partners also knew that we did things for patients' benefit that went way beyond our own interests. Our customers then wanted to support us, as they respected the support we gave them in return. What is key to understand is:

You reap what you sow.

What goes around comes around.

Karma is a beautiful thing. We made our own luck, we sowed well, and were selfless in our pursuit of wellness: our North Star!

Stand out from the pack

Understanding what your customers are actually buying from you is important before considering a purpose statement. The reason for this (highlighted in Chapter 3) is to ensure your purpose statement aligns to customers' real needs, while building trust at the same time.

A lot of organisations rely on product features and benefits to differentiate them from competitors. This will always have limited success, with the constant risk being that someone will come out with better features and benefits. History is littered with examples of when the best product didn't win. The key is not just execution, but *differentiated execution*, which stands out from the pack – and for the right reasons! You need to know your customers well, and understand what they are buying. This links to your purpose statement, which in turn influences your strategies. This then leads to differentiated execution, which is aligned better than anyone else's to your customers' needs.

The key to success is making your offering stand out and the logical choice, even in a crowded, noisy market.

A great example of this is a team I worked with in Asia. They were the market leader, but new competitors were arriving with more convenient options than ours: they wanted to take the No. 1 position.

We recognised from our market knowledge that one of the issues in the therapy area was making sure that patients actually got the drug and took it – this was half the battle. A pure drug supplier wouldn't care: they would supply to the wholesaler, and then it wasn't their problem.

The team turned their sale representatives into project managers, and began partnering with local authorities to ensure this medicine got to the people who needed it. This shifted the team from being a supplier to a real partner. When the tender came up, the team won again – even with competitors offering lower prices for more convenient options. This changed the rules of the game, and the competitors didn't know how to play! They were still just a supplier.

This was fundamental. Speaking with government bodies, it was no longer about the medicine or the price, but about keeping people well. We had shifted their thinking, while the other companies were playing the old game. Reverting to 'just a supplier' would be like going back in time, undoing all the great work that had already been completed.

Understanding the business you're in, then using this in your purpose statement, will change your organisation from being one of the pack to a company that understands and delivers to customers in a unique way, making you untouchable. The head of Revlon cosmetics, Charles Revson, said it so well in this famous quote: 'In the factory we make cosmetics; in the drugstore we sell hope.'[18]

Before we move on, let's summarise where we are at so far:

1. We know and have decided that building a purpose-driven culture can be a game changer for your organisation. We have the focus and courage to follow through and live it every day.

2. We understand the power of possibilities, and ensure the words that we use enable possibilities for our teams. We can spot a downward spiral, and understand that in a world of possibilities, we must provide a trusted alternative.

3. We understand the power of trust and how to diagnose when trust is an issue in a relationship. We also recognise that creating mutual agendas with stakeholders is a game changer for building rock-solid trust and aligned goals.

---

18 'Charles Revson', www.revloninc.com/our-company/our-founders

4. We understand the business we are in, and need to be in. We understand what people are really buying.

We've accomplished so much already – at this point I know you're ready to make changes in your business. This foundation is critical for the next step, so congratulations on making it this far!

Do you know the business you're in?

If you are still not 100% sure of the business you are in, stop here. The easiest way to solve this is to go and talk with your customers: ask them what they value about working with your company. These conversations will either confirm you are right in your thinking, or you may even have another idea.

Next, go and talk to some of your front-line employees and ask them what they think of your ideas. After this, ask your senior leaders. By the end of this process I'm sure you will have confirmed and be clear about the business you are in. It's always good to socialise ideas with people: while the feedback is great, it also helps you to get comfortable asking people questions, as well as being vulnerable and open.

Summary

1. Understanding what business you're in is key, before considering purpose. Are you selling drill bits or holes?

2. Relying on product features and benefits only results in limited long-term success. You cannot always have the latest and best.

3. Understand your customers' frustrations, and help to solve them. This will build a mutual agenda that supports great trust.

4. Talk with your customers, ask them how they use your products, and understand what they value from working with your organisation.

5. Tailoring your organisation around your customers' needs will ensure your execution is differentiated and better aligned to their needs.

5

Build Your Purpose

It's time to talk purpose! We're now ready, as we have a mindset of possibilities, understand the importance of trust and, importantly, understand what customers are really buying. Purpose becomes the lens through which all strategies and initiatives are focused. This has power for two reasons:

- It differentiates your execution, allowing you to stand out from the crowd

- It ensures your execution is aligned to your customers' deep-rooted needs and desires – not the face-value need, but the underlying, true motivation.

For example, when people buy an iPhone, are they buying an easy-to-use communication device, or are they buying into Apple design, thinking differently and the status of having the latest iPhone? Logically, it is a communications device, but it's also everything else. This is why iPhone advertising is designed to show off the beauty of design and imagery, rather than talking about technical specifications. It isn't logic, but inspiring people to want to buy.

Remember Donald Calne's words about emotion leading to actions (Chapter 2)?

Before we begin, let's understand how a purpose statement differs from a mission or vision statement. A vision or mission is a company's ambition set well into the future. It is created to set the tone and inspire people. In my experience, mission or vision statements don't drive any action: if you investigate most of these companies, the day-to-day running is more about meeting quarterly targets than achieving the vision.

Let's look at two examples. American Express uses 'We work hard every day to make American Express the world's most respected service brand' and Patagonia goes with 'Build the best product, cause no unnecessary harm, use business to inspire and implement solutions to the environmental crisis'.

While these are aspirational, they are high level: they talk about the company rather than the people they are serving. Especially Patagonia – 'build the best product, cause no unnecessary harm'? These are internally focused and things that customers would expect from any company.

For a purpose to be powerful it must talk about your ambition for your customers.

Building a purpose statement

A purpose statement speaks to the reason an organisation exists right now. It should speak to employees about the organisation's aspirations for customers. As discussed in the previous chapter, it's about understanding what people are really buying from you. Let's look at Starbucks: while it has a purpose statement, it links also to its mission. Starbucks' *mission* is 'to inspire and nurture the human spirit – one person, one cup and one neighborhood at a time' while its *purpose* is 'to establish Starbucks as the premier purveyor of the finest coffee in the world while maintaining our uncompromising principles while we grow'.

The Starbucks statement has begun to do this with the combination of mission and purpose. To nurture the human spirit goes beyond coffee: it speaks to why people want a coffee; you see this when someone takes the first sip of their favourite drink. Their eyes close, there is a smile on their face and you can feel how that first sip takes them to a different place. That's the experience they want for their customers. Starbucks has shown this desire to inspire and nurture by launching Starbucks Reserve™ Roastery, a premium version of Starbucks that speaks to its mission.

STARBUCKS SHANGHAI RESERVE ROASTERY

The Shanghai store is a visual sensation, selling everything related to coffee including coffee-making equipment, as well as food and beer. Coffee is available from a coffee machine, pour-over syphon or cold brew. It is inspirational. This store is a result of Starbucks' thinking beyond brewing coffee and puts their purpose into action.

On their website they use the words 'dream', 'passion' and 'ambition' to describe what they are aiming for. This is demonstrated by the team who work there: they are passionate about the coffee and the experience, they wear their beautiful aprons with pride, and you can see it from the look on their faces. You're not just buying a flat white, you are buying artistry and experience. The coffee will taste better just for this reason, nothing more. Not logic, not spreadsheets – they are nurturing the human soul.

I was talking with a new client in the compliance business. When I asked what their customers really wanted, they said, 'We just want to pass their audits and have no issues.'

I said, 'But what do they really want?' It took many 'yes and' comments to get deeper. It finished with considering how to create competitive advantage by making it faster and more efficient to remain compliant: 'We've got your back.'

While it's still early days, they are seeing their customers and solutions differently now – well beyond just getting through the next audit. That's what their competitors do. They now have their customers' backs, building better systems and working with customers to show compliance in a more efficient way.

As discussed previously, when working in pharma our purpose statement was: 'An Unstoppable Drive to Restore People's Lives.' 'Restore life' speaks to the reason for being, but also the desire of anyone living with a disability or disease. 'Restore life' allowed team members to think more expansively about how to do this. 'Unstoppable' drove the team to fight hurdles, so as to keep bringing new and innovative initiatives to life. This purpose statement was balanced and inspiring, but also extremely clear about the desired outcome: grounded and customer-focused.

Everyone in an organisation should be able to say and see how and what they do is helping the company achieve its purpose. When building a great purpose statement, these are the qualities and focus areas to bring together:

1. What's your ambition for your customers, based on what they are really buying?

2. What are the unique values of your organisation and the way you execute?

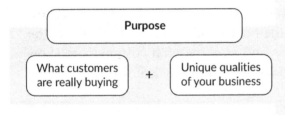

Purpose statement formula

This will be the foundation for everything going forward; it's the genesis. This statement will inspire you and your teams every day to bounce out of bed and go to work! Importantly, also having integrated this into your organisation, it will resonate with your customers: 'I want to work with this company!'

Get senior leaders involved

Before getting on to the purpose statement, two final questions we need to ask are:

- How much time does our leadership team spend in the field?
- How close are they to the front line of the business?

If the answers to these questions are 'little' and 'not very close', you need to get your senior leaders out there for a couple of days with a list of questions they can ask your front-line team and customers. The following examples are designed as conversation starters: it's important for your senior people to go out with aligned questions, so the team can discuss the answers when they return.

Questions for front-line staff

- What is the biggest challenge you have executing in your role every day?

- If you could change one thing about the product or service that would help you with customers, what would it be?

- What is your motivation to come to work each day?

- What challenges do you see in the next two to three years?

Questions for your customers

- What do you enjoy about working with our organisation?

- What is the biggest challenge you are facing in your role?

- What frustrates you about working with our organisation?

Limit the number of questions, but try to get as many answers as you can for each question. Once you have all the responses, collate the results. The answers will help ground your senior leaders with the current issues and challenges in your organisation, and understand your customers' current needs and desires.

Run a workshop

Now you're ready to run a purpose workshop with your senior leaders: it will take most of a day. You should use an external facilitator, but it must be the senior leaders who work together to create a purpose they believe in. You cannot just get management consultants to do it for you, otherwise you have no buy-in or belief in the purpose – and it will not be your truth, as the consultants don't necessarily know what that is.

Begin the workshop by going through the feedback from the fieldwork, then discuss as a team the insights from the answers to the questions you asked your customers, as well as any personal observations.

Then, through the workshop process, discuss the business you are in, and what your customers are really buying from you. Also, understand your organisation's values:

- What are your leaders proud of?

- What do they think sets you apart from your competitors?

Understanding this will help you bring together the components in a way that is linked already to who you are as an organisation. It also ensures that the purpose statement is grounded in some truth. This is important, that there is truth or demonstration to some part of the purpose statement. If you write something that is so foreign to where your organisation is, you will have trouble getting your teams to believe in it. It can become a joke, so try to take part of what you are proud of and include this in the purpose.

When I did this with my organisation, we worked with the person from the agency, (discussed in Chapter 1). In pharma we understood that our role needed to shift from being a supplier of drugs to a supplier of wellness. That was the result our doctors and the government payer were looking for. We knew that if we did this better than our competitors, the patients on our products would get a better outcome, and doctors would then prefer to prescribe our products. This gave us a great competitive advantage.

The 'Unstoppable Drive' came from how we were working as a business: we were getting things done where others had failed; we kept trying until we found a way. We were unstoppable, and the team really related to this concept.

One of the other key insights we had from speaking to patients was that when you have a condition or disease, people's aspirations change – they just dream of and strive to live a normal life – so 'restoring lives' seemed like a perfect way to say this. This also spoke to the government payer, who was looking to make people well and keep people working and contributing to society.

I couldn't have imagined how powerful this purpose was, for both myself and my team. We began to think differently about everything. The scope of our work significantly increased. With patient programmes, wellness became the goal, which changed what we wanted to offer: we understood wellness was not just physical, but also psychological and emotional.

Working through the lens of wellness with patients, we found opportunities to support people well beyond traditional offerings. An example of this came from another insight. When people are diagnosed with a condition, often they don't want to speak with a loved one, health professional or even a counsellor: they want to talk with others living with the same condition. This drove our team to build an online community to facilitate this: it was a huge success; we had patients feeling that the community did as much as the medicine to help them recover. The community was so supportive; it was amazing to see the beauty of humanity and people caring for each other. People from all walks of life united together with a desire to help each other make tomorrow a better day.

While creating an online community may not seem revolutionary, it was for a pharma company. This was a nightmare for our compliance and legal teams, who to begin with said it couldn't be done. The power now came from our purpose and the intent and reason for building the community. To begin, we spent lots of time talking to people about our 'Unstoppable Drive to Restore People's Lives', and how people wanted to talk with others living with the same condition. We were able to get everyone inspired by the dream of what we wanted to create.

Compliance and legal became supporters when they bought into the intention. They started to help us navigate the challenges to bring the community to life. With each challenge the team would sit and discuss how we could solve it.

It took time, but we did it.

Before we close this chapter, some of you may be thinking, 'But my organisation doesn't do anything noble! We just make widgets which no one cares about.' I agree – it is more of a challenge, but rest assured it's not impossible.

Differentiate from competitors

Here is a great example which shows how a company selling female hygiene products created purpose and differentiated itself from its competitors. This example was a campaign, but it could have been integrated into a great purpose-driven culture, sustainable for years to come.

#THROWLIKEAGIRL

Go to YouTube, search for 'throw like a girl' and watch the video – it's fantastic.[19] The producer asks two age groups to 'throw like a girl'. The first group, teenagers and young adult girls and boys, pretend to be all stupid and limp. They then ask five-to-ten-year-old girls to do the same, and they try their hardest to do their best. The video demonstrates how there is a change in what 'throw like a girl' means for different age groups. The young ones try their hardest, and the older ones think 'like a girl' is a joke.

---

19 'Always like a girl', www.youtube.com/watch?v=XjJQBjWYDTs

The question is: 'When did throwing like a girl become an insult?'

This is a powerful and emotive recording, and few who see it are likely to use the expression 'like a girl' in a derogatory way again. The video was created by the hygiene brand Always, standing up for women and highlighting the importance of self-esteem.

How powerful is that! A female hygiene company is changing the world for the better for women. Can you imagine a person selling their products versus a competitor? They can stand proud in comparison with their competitors. Imagine you're in an aisle in the supermarket: which product would you choose?

This is such a great example: think of the purpose statement that could come from this. For your organisation, maybe your widget is pretty uninspiring, but there is always something related to your organisation and product which could be inspirational: a purpose your organisation can get behind.

TESLA: WHERE THERE'S A WILL, THERE'S A WAY

Tesla's execution and charging method is unique and a differentiator. Currently, Tesla cars are differentiated, but other motor manufacturers are catching up. Tesla has its own simple charging stations which are easier to use, while all other manufacturers rely on third-party charging stations that require people to belong to different networks and carry their own cables.

Buying a Tesla is like buying an appliance online: it is delivered to you. The company doesn't have traditional showrooms, but shops on the high street. Combined with the charging outlets that it is installing all over the world, Tesla cars are easy to buy and charge, and the buying experience isn't at a car dealership, which most people don't like.

Buying online also makes the pricing standard: everyone pays the same, which gives peace of mind at purchase. Let's face it, negotiating for a car is a pain – we only do it because we hate to think we're paying more than someone else.

It doesn't matter that competitors come out with similar cars; Tesla has points of differentiation that set it apart.

Expanding the purpose statement

Customer ambition = Restoring life

Unique organisation qualities = Unstoppable drive

Once you have your purpose statement, congratulations! You're about to embark on an amazing journey. From the purpose statement you then need to create an explanation no longer than one page, in large font. Use all the notes from the workshop to flesh this out.

This one page should be all that anyone needs to read to understand your business and your team's ambition: it explains your customer ambition + unique organisation qualities in more detail.

This will become a wall poster, so new people or guests in your office can quickly read what your organisation stands for and what it's working to achieve. At this point you might be thinking: 'Should it be that public?' The answer is yes. It has no value unless everyone knows and experiences it. It also shows your team that you are proud of it.

You might also be thinking, 'But competitors could copy it now, we would lose our advantage.' Remember that the purpose statement has to be your truth? You are right though: competitors will come in and think, 'Wow, we need to make one of these statement thingies.' But their focus will be on the statement, while yours is on living it. These are two extremely different things.

My 'Unstoppable Drive to Restore People's Lives' poster and explanation was in our reception area, also in our boardroom. Often, we would hold industry meetings with our competitors, and let doctors use our meeting rooms. They all got to see what we stood for, and understood why we did what we did.

Interestingly, our explanation specifically called out our government payer by name and our ambition to make them our advocate. We had our payer come to meetings: it was right there in front of them.

Actions speak louder than words. You have to be brave and proud of your purpose statement, and put it where everyone can see it – you will find it easier to live the purpose when it's everywhere. Socialising ideas is powerful: your team will be socialising what you stand for and what you do. This is how purpose becomes the norm in an organisation.

In my case, the word 'unstoppable' became the language of our organisation. Whenever there were challenges or hurdles to overcome, people would say, 'But we are unstoppable!' – it drove them to find a way. It meant they couldn't give up at the first hurdle, and made the challenge fun. I was actually given a t-shirt with 'Unstoppable' written on it!

This became the DNA of our culture, and made us invincible. Customers would say they were pleased to work with us, as they knew whatever we needed to do, we would never let them down.

Remember: people won't believe what you say, they will believe in what you do. You must be intentional.

The power of trust and purpose

When you combine purpose and trust, you are likely to find that there is greater scope for openness and transparency with staff and customers. It often scares people when I mention this, as there may be much that they would rather not share with their customers.

Can you imagine how this could increase the trustworthiness of your organisation?

This may also be liberating for both you and your teams. If you ask your people, you may find that one of the biggest frustrations they experience is when they believe a task in their role undermines their integrity. This is especially true when front-line teams building relationships with customers are told by marketing to say or do something to customers with which they don't agree, or when they are having to say different things to different people in certain situations.

Setting your organisation on a path to more openness and transparency will be refreshing for everyone, and another gesture that shows your resolve to live your purpose. If the integrity of the organisation and that of your team is sound, you have nothing to hide.

Summary

1. Before creating your purpose, make sure your senior leaders are close enough to the business.

2. Ensure that you're clear about the business you are in, and what customers buy from you.

3. Consider what is already unique about your organisation and team.

4. Workshop with a mindset of possibilities and knowledge of your customers.

5. Your purpose statement should combine your ambition for your customers and what is unique about your organisation, and help employees understand this.

6. Ensure your purpose statement is visible throughout your organisation by printing it and posting it on the walls.

6

'DUMB' Goals Kill 'SMART' Goals

Intrigued? If you have not heard of DUMB goals before, read on.[20]

Deep down you know that making goals SMART – specific, measurable, achievable, realistic and time-bound – is sometimes necessary, but it sucks the life out of you. It's like going to the dentist: no one wants to or looks forward to it, but they know they have to so they just do it.

SMART goals are like that: obviously they do have a place, and definitely around incentives and bonuses. But if you consider high achievers in the world,

---

20 Brendon Burchard, 'How NOT to Set Goals (Why S.M.A.R.T. goals are lame)', www.youtube.com/watch?v=54aFTZ9POw4&t=11s

none of them would have set SMART goals. Can you imagine Steve Jobs or Bill Gates doing this? They have goals, but always big ones – plus they have the discipline to follow through on them. The challenge with setting goals is that the focus is way too narrow, the result generally binary – success or failure – and the time frame often limited to a year.

For these reasons, SMART goals have no place in strategy unless you are happy with suboptimal performance. For strategy you want 'DUMB' goals – yes, the opposite of SMART ones.

Anatomy of the DUMB goal

For high-performing teams, the DUMB goal structure provides a fantastic process for working out the team goal. In the past I have seen goals that people initially thought impossible actually being achieved.

What is a DUMB goal? It is:

• **D**ream-driven

• **U**plifting

• **M**ethod-friendly

• **B**ehaviour-driven

Dream-driven

This is the exciting part. I would ask teams the question: 'What's your rocking-chair achievement for this team?'

Imagine you are talking with a young child and telling them about this amazing team you were in: what is it that you and the team achieved? This is a time for expansionist thinking: not to think about the how, but to decide the big goal: 'We choose to go to the Moon.'

You may want to consider the time frame, and what you will have achieved by then; three years has worked well for me. That kind of time frame seems appropriate for a big goal; but having the goal so big may mean that even the first steps are not clear.

For example, if you think of the launch team I was leading (in Chapter 1), their goal was to navigate a winning course to achieve funding for the product. This may not sound big and as-pirational, but at that point it was very much a dream, given the environment in which we were operating.

This team had nothing working in their favour and a competitor who seemed to hold all the cards. The confirmation that this was definitely

> a dream is that everyone on that team now uses this story as their rocking-chair moment – the time we beat all the odds and won. It was truly an inspirational story that would not have happened without the DUMB goal.

Uplifting

This will seem logical, but the way you write this goal must be positive. When someone reads this goal, they should say: 'Wow, that's awesome!' It wouldn't be right to have a goal such as: 'We will destroy our competitor and become number one.' This is negative and one that most likely you wouldn't want anyone else to know. You want your teams to be proud of their goal and inspired: when they are telling people what it is, they should become excited just talking about it.

Remember to live with your 'possibilities' mindset – it will serve you well in writing the goal.

Method-friendly

Method-friendly is the most important part of the DUMB goal process, and brings the power to teams. Method-friendly is what your teams will spend most of their time doing.

With a dream goal established, we don't yet know the path to achieve it. The method is all about working out what you are going to start doing to uncover the *how*: the engine room to achieve the DUMB goal, what makes the dream a reality.

To begin to help your teams, consider these questions:

- What would the conditions need to be for you to achieve the goal?
- What changes would need to happen?
- What would stakeholders need to think and believe?

Once this is established, consider where the stakeholders are now: this gap is what your teams will need to close over time.

The methods are what your teams should be constantly thinking about now: what could we try? When they begin making progress: what have we learned so far, how does this change things?

When your team is in this mindset and having discussions with various people, ideas will come up which the team can brainstorm. You will also find when discussing ideas with your stakeholders that many will want to help and support you.

Stay focused on the methods, and progress will begin to happen.

For example, the Asia team example from Chapter 4 started with a tender which focused purely on price.

Current position	Delta	Future state
Purely price-focused	The methods need to bridge the gap from current to future	Recognised value beyond price

The method for this team was about understanding how they could change mindset to consider more than price: the desired future state. This was the focus for the team, to differentiate their offering beyond cost, as they knew they couldn't win on this alone – it would be a race to the bottom. They achieved this by changing their business model and providing the value of making sure that medication got to the people who needed it. They won the tender without competing on price. Documenting the current position versus the future state helped the team focus on how to bridge the gap between the two. They won the tender with a higher price by achieving the future state above.

Behaviour-driven

When you are starting this process, behaviours are important. As we've already seen, in most organisations today, people are programmed to think about risk and live in a downward spiral: a comfortable but soul-destroying place to be. Behaviours are where we bring our mindset of possibilities to life. We need our team to be positive, committed to finding opportunities and staying focused on the goal.

If the team is an established one which has been meeting in the past, it's likely that their meetings will have been information-sharing discussions by individuals in a group; they won't have been actively working to achieve something. If this is the case it's important that, after a high-performing teams workshop and the establishment of a DUMB goal, they don't return to the organisation and continue to operate as before. People need to realise that there is a line in the sand. From this point, things will be different: the focus is the goal and working together to uncover the methods to achieve it.

Get your teams to meet somewhere different than before – change things up so that they recognise the shift from the past – otherwise it will be too easy to fall back into old ways. The team leader plays a crucial role of keeping people *on* track and helping them transition to new ways of working.

That's the DUMB goals process. Big goals are so important: without the big goal, no one is focused on achieving anything more than day-to-day tasks. Goals also unite a team around a single focus. The DUMB method ensures the goal is exciting, worthwhile and will drive your organisation forward.

Remember to celebrate the progress your teams are making. The journey is more important than the end result, and celebrating success along the way keeps everyone motivated, inspired and engaged.

You may also want to consider a personal DUMB goal. (Writing this book is actually mine: English was my worst subject at school and I think I may be dyslexic, so this was a big goal. If you are reading this, I'm pretty proud!)

Imagine the difference in organisations focused on SMART versus DUMB goals. SMART goal organisations will be looking for small incremental increases: when setting SMART goals, the natural reaction is to aim low. I know from my own experience that I would never look at my SMART goals until the end of the year. They weren't a personal driver.

The push on time-bound goals and needing to achieve them within a specific time frame means that people are always focused on the short term, and are never thinking big or in the long term. In most cases, if you are working in an organisation, everyone's days are filled with process, meetings and procedure, allowing little time to think and strategise about the future. The focus is on just getting through. Companies like this have internalised everything and are likely to miss market shifts, as these aren't their area of attention.

Companies with DUMB goals have all their teams actively working on the future, trying to change the game and coming up with innovative ideas. People and teams will be finding efficiencies to get the day-to-day done, so that they can help their teams to elevate to the exciting projects that achieve their DUMB goal.

Such a contrast, isn't it? If you go around your organisation, are people's days filled with day-to-day activities, or can you find teams actively working to achieve a big goal?

> If you want to be happy, set a goal that commands your thoughts, liberates your energy and inspires your hopes.
> — Andrew Carnegie

In the next chapter we will look at how to incorporate DUMB goals into your teams.

Summary

1. DUMB goals provide a framework to build and drive ambitious goals for your customers.

2. Imagine the rocking chair story to inspire your ambition. Don't worry about the how, just think what would be awesome to achieve.

3. Method is how we uncover the path to achieve the goal. This should be the team's focus.

4. Understanding your stakeholders' current belief versus the belief required to achieve the goal will help you understand the gap you need to fill.

5. A combination of possibilities and attention to the DUMB goal ensures that people stay focused on the ambition, and continue to think about the how.

7

Building Teams

> Great discoveries and achievements invariably involve
> the cooperation of many minds.
> — Alexander Graham Bell

Teams need to be built – they don't just happen!
There has been lots of research on their power. Set
up correctly, teams can produce results well beyond
what could have been achieved as individuals. Building a purpose-driven culture starts with teams. They
are the link from purpose to strategy: set them up for
success, and work to ensure the strategies they create
are aligned to the company's purpose.

Your teams are the power base of the organisation,
so appreciating how to create high-performing ones

needs to become part of its understanding. The art has been lost over time: these days, team-building often consists of an evening of, say, ten pin bowling followed by drinks at a pub. While bowling helps build morale, it doesn't build the necessary qualities for a high-performing team.

So, what makes a high-performing team and how is this different from your current teams? The definition I used to measure teams against is this:

> A group of people who are responsible for the creation of an ambitious strategy and who are actively *working together to achieve it.*

The key here is: people working together to achieve a common goal.

If you consider some of your teams, would you say they are doing that? The easiest way to check this is to look at meeting agendas: are they division or departmental updates, or workshops of ideas and updates on feedback from a new strategy? The power of a team is the collective value of everyone thinking, solving problems and creating opportunities together. If the agenda is just divisional updates, this is a group of individuals informing others about what they are doing.

Understanding what constitutes a high-performing team is important: with time you will be able to immediately recognise one.

The Drexler/Sibbet Team Performance Model®

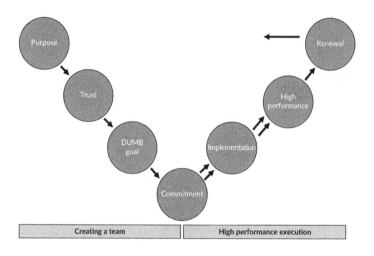

My version of a high-performing team model adapted from the Drexler/Sibbet model

I was introduced to the Drexler/Sibbet Team Performance Model®[21] through a leaders' programme. When I investigated further, I found it follows the logical steps we all take when joining a team. The model provides a great structure for building teams,

---

21   https://davidsibbet.com/process-models

which I have used for many years. For simplicity and understanding, consider the first four qualities – needed to create your team (the other three qualities; implementation, high performance and renewal – will be looked at later in the chapter).

The model follows what people joining a team will generally think.

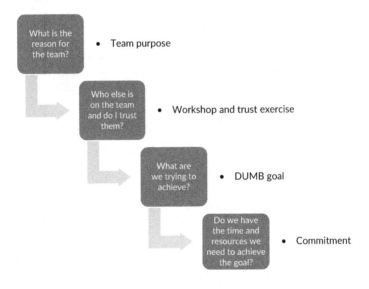

What is the reason for the team? • Team purpose

Who else is on the team and do I trust them? • Workshop and trust exercise

What are we trying to achieve? • DUMB goal

Do we have the time and resources we need to achieve the goal? • Commitment

Natural thought process when joining a team

Note the V-shape of the Drexler/Sibbet model: it represents how grounded each quality is. When considering the team purpose, this can be high level, aspirational and full of possibilities; as you go further down, the more grounded the quality becomes.

Then consider trust: again, you cannot touch it – it's how people feel; it's not tangible. When you get to commitment, the requirements are more tangible: do we have the time and resources required to be successful? This is where the rubber meets the road: from commitment there is a bounce to implementation, then high performance. Again, high performance is not tangible – it's a feeling, a level of excitement. This means that when building teams, we begin high level and become more grounded; once there, momentum provides the bounce back up to implementation and high performance.

When you form any team, the first task should be to sit down and craft the team purpose together, understand and get to know your teammates, decide on a goal, then allocate the necessary time and resource to enable the team to execute successfully. The order of the qualities is also important: getting the purpose and trust established is vital before a team can consider the goal. It goes without saying that if you don't know the purpose of the team, you can't work out the goal.

Purpose

While the organisation has a purpose, which could be used here, in most cases it makes sense to narrow the purpose to the group's responsibilities. There should always be alignment between the organisation and team: this is fundamental, and the way to make sure of a strong link between the company purpose and the team strategies.

Purpose, like all the qualities, must be worked on together as a team. Setting the purpose is often overlooked by people, as they assume everyone knows why they are there; but if you ask each person the question 'Why are you here?', they would all have different answers. Setting this up first provides everyone on the team with clarity and an opportunity for alignment.

Trust

We have already covered the importance of trust and the Trust Equation in Chapter 3. Relationships need trust, which is why teams also must have trust to function.

The focus of trust in the Drexler/Sibbet model is about ensuring that everyone on the team knows each other and understands what they contribute. This is about inclusion and ensuring that people have a bond, which means they can be themselves within the team and feel comfortable to challenge when they don't agree.

In my experience, the quality of trust in a team environment directly correlates to the quality of the team's output. When trust is challenged, people immediately switch back to being an individual, only contributing when requested. As a team leader, you always need to be watching the team interacting, to ensure the foundation of trust remains.

It is important, though, not to misunderstand disagreement as challenging trust. When there is a strong bond of trust in a team, people will feel comfortable to challenge each other, as they know the person has the right intentions: the issue is not personal, but about achieving the best result. This is positive – you want people to challenge each other constructively.

In these sorts of situations, always try to achieve consensus by the close of the meeting and end on something positive. Also, highlight to the team the importance of robust discussion. Importantly, by the time everyone leaves they should be smiling and still getting along. Managing trust as a leader is crucial, as it can be the biggest derailer

Consider the Trust Equation now. Imagine you are in a team where people do not follow through (reliability) and are only interested in their own department's tasks (self-orientation). Your natural response is to pull back and not contribute either – you're going to question why you are there. You are back at 'purpose' in the model. This is a great demonstration of how you can apply the Trust Equation to different challenges.

DUMB Goal

Here, we insert the DUMB goals process from Chapter 6. The role and focus of the team from this point forward is to actively work together to create the goal, and to discover how to achieve it. As outlined previously, in DUMB goals this is the method: what is the team going to do to find the path to achieve their goal?

The goal should be ambitious, with a time frame of two to three years. A big goal will excite, align and focus the team.

Commitment

After identifying the goal, the team must decide how much time they need to allocate working together on the 'how'.

- Will they need additional resources or help?
- Will they meet monthly or perhaps fortnightly?
- Where will they meet?

While these aspects may seem like common sense, decisions upfront align everyone in agreement and are incredibly important.

When a team gets to this point, they are excited, inspired and, while committed, are not confident they can do it. People are focused and want to play a role in helping the team achieve the goal, but it can seem overwhelming and people are often unsure as to how they will achieve it. Their confidence will grow as you begin implementing new ideas and making progress. At this point you have formed a team. Everyone is agreed and aligned on the purpose, people trust each other, and a big goal is set. The team is now ready to actively work together to achieve the goal.

This is the power of a team: it is now formed and ready to go!

As per the model, the next steps are:

- Implementation
- High performance
- Renewal

Implementation

Once the team is established, the first few months are vital. As its leader, you play an important role in keeping them focused and looking for possibilities. In my experience, during the months after, people will come up with ideas and bring them to the team; they also may have gone away and investigated some initial ideas. The team will work through these and build on them to achieve success.

Out of these ideas the team will begin to implement, and this is where the magic happens. The results of the first initiatives come in: likely the majority will be successful and the team will uncover something new they had not considered before. With this momentum, the team is now making progress to achieve what only a few months ago seemed an impossible dream.

High performance

As mentioned earlier at the commitment stage, while people are committed, they are not completely confident that they can do it. With progress being made through implementation, they are now excited about what's next and becoming more confident that they can achieve the goal. There is an energy in the team, people are looking forward to meetings.

This is high performance; the team is now constantly thinking of possibilities, coming up with more innovative ideas from what they have learned from their initial implementations. Being in a high-performing team is a great place to be – this is a time that people will remember forever. As an organisation, if you have your teams operating at this level, there is nothing stopping you. Your team will be executing faster with more exciting projects, all aligned to helping you achieve the company purpose together. People will see you as a great leader. Your sole focus should be supporting your team leaders to keep the teams at a high-performing level.

Renewal

This step in the model is all about repeating the process, but what this means in practical terms is that as the leader of a team, you must ensure that the first four qualities of purpose, trust, goal and commitment remain active at all times. The minute that any one of these qualities is lost, the team will shift from high performance to questioning the purpose or why they are there. They will revert to being individuals.

When you look at research and *Harvard Business Review* articles, such as Laura Delizonna's *HBR* article discussing safety in teams, or Dr Tim Baker's LinkedIn article detailing the '8 Characteristics of High Performing Teams', you will find lots of different models or studies highlighting the qualities for high-performing teams.[22, 23] All of them say the same thing in different ways.

The power of the Drexler/Sibbet model is its simplicity and that it gives us a structure and order for how to build a team, and allows us to understand how we think when we become part of a team.

22 L Delizonna, 'High-performing teams need psychological safety. Here's how to create it', *Harvard Business Review*, 2017, https://hbr. org/2017/08/high-performing-teams-need-psychological-safety-heres-how-to-create-it
23 T Baker, 'The 8 characteristics of high performing teams', LinkedIn, 2018, www.linkedin.com/pulse/8-characteristics-high-performing-teams-dr-tim-baker

The key is: regardless of the model, when establishing a team, time needs to be set aside to align it and get everyone on board.

Google spent two years researching 180 teams to understand what makes teams successful.[24] The conclusion was that there were five traits to high-performing teams:

1. Dependability

2. Structure and clarity

3. Meaning

4. Impact

5. Psychological safety

When you read this research, you will recognise that these qualities are all covered in the Drexler/Sibbet model.

Summary

1. Understand the basic principles of the Drexler/ Sibbet model and learn to apply them in a way that suits your teams and your organisation.

---

24 J Rozovsky, 'The five keys to a successful Google team', re:Work, 2015, https://rework.withgoogle.com/blog/five-keys-to-a-successful-google-team

2. Recognise that teams need to be built; they don't just happen.

3. 'Actively working together' is the difference between a team and a group of individuals.

4. High performance is achieved through successful implementation of new strategies. You will begin to see a level of excitement in the team, as they begin to achieve success.

5. To maintain high performance, the team's purpose and goal must remain relevant, and trust must be maintained at all times.

8
Unleashing The Power Of Teams

This is all about maintaining the qualities that keep teams performing. Nothing ever stands still, so maintaining your teams is more important than the initial work to create them. As mentioned previously, it's all about keeping team purpose and trust alive, focusing on the DUMB goal and commitment to following through. Too often, people spend time focusing on establishing the team, but after a few months it can revert to old ways. Teams watch their leader to learn how to act, as this is new for everyone, so the leader plays a critical role.

Leaders need to understand how to handle new team additions (more on this below), and how to maintain focus in challenging times. Organisations need to recognise the importance of team leadership. This chapter focuses on how organisations can support their leaders.

The first time I used the Drexler/Sibbet model, I was leading a team and we had our first team meeting, which was a disaster. Everyone was talking over one another, different agendas coming from different functions – it was a mess! Don't get me wrong, it was a group of highly talented people, but they were all working as individuals and believed that what they were doing was more important than anything else.

We set aside two days and brought the team together to review purpose, trust, goal and commitment. At the end of this exercise I was amazed at the transformation – the alignment, camaraderie – people quickly understood the need to work together. What they realised is that all their different functional initiatives were important, but without alignment to the broader strategy, their impact would be significantly less. The team now understood that to be successful, they needed to work together, to be strategic and aligned when executing the strategy. They realised that before they were only focused on functional day-to-day activities which, while important, were now the expectation and not the purpose of team meetings.

This team achieved significant success beyond what they initially imagined. They won business which, two years prior, some would have said was impossible.

Interestingly, this team achieved their goal and were high-performing, but then we didn't establish a new goal and the team broke down. In the eyes of other people within the organisation, they became 'cocky' or 'arrogant'. Within eighteen months, most of the team had left the organisation.

This shows the importance of keeping all the qualities in check. Without a new goal the team lost its way, impacting its performance. The reason so many of the team left the organisation was they were searching for the magic they had once felt while working in a high-performance environment. Once people experience this in a purpose-driven culture, it is extremely difficult to return to work for a pay cheque or the everyday.

Still, the spirit and inspiration of this time lives in the hearts of the people who achieved what

> seemed to be impossible. This group still meets for dinner occasionally; they have a bond which will last a lifetime.

I cannot emphasise enough the power of high-performing teams with a big goal. All the leaders in your organisation need to understand the basic principles of the Drexler/Sibbet model by heart.

As mentioned previously, it is key to make the link from purpose to strategy. Without high-performing teams with big goals aligned to the purpose, your purpose statement will never become part of your organisation's DNA. Teams who are high-performing and make the link are naturally innovative: with ambition comes the need for innovation; it just happens. You will be able to laugh at the companies who say their focus is on innovation! Without ambition, what are people innovating – better paperclips?

Unleash your teams, set them up for success, and you will be astonished at their execution.

New team additions

In most cases in organisations, people come and go. New people are brought in, and others leave. You can imagine it doesn't make sense to redo a high-performing team workshop each time a team member joins – new people just need to be onboarded. The team leader should take them through:

- The team purpose

- Who is in the team

- The goal of the team

- The progress they are making

At the next meeting, set aside some time for introductions, so you can begin to build the bond of trust between the new person and the rest of the group.

Once you are aligned with this model, stick with it and it will become embedded in your organisation. There will always be new research which gets picked up by the media or business commentators. This has happened to me over the years, and every time I have investigated, I have found no new data which has brought anything new or challenged the validity of the Drexler/Sibbet model.

Stick with one model

With a focus on the team, your leaders may be hungering for more information too. It's important to stick with the Drexler/Sibbet model and not be swayed by new bright and shiny models and research, as they will all be similar. You want everyone to be working off the same structure, so that it becomes natural.

To show how all models are similar, let's look again at the Google research (see the previous chapter) to make the link between its qualities and the Drexler/Sibbet model:

Google	Drexler/Sibbet model
Dependability	Trust
Structure and clarity	Goal
Meaning	Purpose
Impact	Commitment/Purpose
Psychological safety	Trust

You will note that I have repeated some of the Drexler/Sibbet qualities against Google. For example, trust provides both dependability and psychological safety.

Don't get hung-up on models and more research. I've already outlined that they all amount to the same thing. By using Drexler/Sibbet and sticking with it, all your teams will understand it, and it will simply become a way of working. Let your teams fly!

Get senior leader buy-in

Lastly, for high-performing teams to succeed, they must be supported by senior leaders and given the power, authority and latitude to develop and execute their plans. They must have the authority to change the game.

It doesn't work if the team's strategies are second-guessed by functional department heads. This completely undermines the team; it will never be successful. Your leadership team must be aligned to empowering your high-performing team: if issues arise, leadership should collectively consider the issue and if change is needed, one of the leadership team should talk to the team leader and explain why. By doing this, you may find with greater context, and a better understanding of the intention, that a solution can be found – which means the team and functions can move forward in better alignment.

As the team leader, recognise that when you are empowering teams, you or someone on your leadership team may not always like the outcomes or ideas that the team brings up. You need to get used to this, and enjoy the team challenging your leadership team.

For greater understanding of this, McKinsey & Company have an article on their website, 'Unleashing the power of small, independent teams', that highlights this well.[25] The article challenges leaders to let go of outdated command and control behaviours and structures; the success of teams depends on it. They should recognise that teams cannot overcome bureaucratic challenges themselves.

If, for example, senior leaders were constantly overriding team decisions, eventually the teams become frustrated and give up. The focus will become politics and not strategy development and execution.

In the Appendix you will also find a workshop guide to building high-performing teams.

Once you have put in place the qualities of a high-performing team – purpose, trust, DUMB goal and commitment – the focus for teams will be on finding the path to achieve the DUMB goal. This should be the sole focus and will help you cut initiatives that are not aligned. Organisations without a strong drive to achieving a big goal appear seriously busy executing things which, in isolation, seem like a good idea. When you have a goal, it will be clear that the initiatives you decide on will be the ones that help you progress closer to the goal.

---

25   O Bossert et al, 'Unleashing the power of small, independent teams', McKinsey Quarterly, 2018, www.mckinsey.com/business-functions/organization/our-insights/unleashing-the-power-of-small-independent-teams

Be confident

At this point you might be thinking, 'Hang on – in the Trust chapter I was told to be interested in others' agenda, now I'm being told to be extremely focused?' When I say 'stay extremely focused', I mean *internally* focused. In most organisations you could drop 60% of initiatives and your customers wouldn't care, or may not even notice. Just stay focused on high-performing team qualities and keeping the team moving forward to achieve the goal. Working together, the team will create the right initiatives.

Remember: the organisation's purpose will highlight your ambition to customers. This cascades to the team purpose, and in turn to the DUMB goal. With this clear link, your team's ambition will benefit your customers and stakeholders. This is why it is so important that the purpose includes the customers' ambition. It will ensure your organisation is both customer- and outward-focused.

After setting the DUMB goal you are likely to feel a little stressed and scared, worried that you cannot make it happen. This is natural to begin with. The team is also not sure they can do it. With the team, you have to be confident and passionate. This is the leadership challenge; the team need to see your confidence in them. Trust me when I tell you: you will be surprised how quickly the team begins to make progress. You will be inspired by the ideas your team brings up. This quote attributed to Nelson Mandela is very apt: 'It always seems impossible until it's done.'

Manage momentum

After the workshop is complete, as with launching a purpose statement, actions speak louder than words. You are taking your team into a new way of thinking and working; they will be unclear and look to you to understand how these changes should impact how they operate. As mentioned previously, while the workshop has your team at 'commitment' in the Drexler/Sibbet model, this will be something completely new for them. They will be committed but not confident; they won't be sure that the team can achieve the goal.

This is a time for your leadership to inspire confidence and determination in both the goal and the team. You must believe in yourself and your team; lead by example. This belief is important as people will see it in you when you talk. Keep the team focused and stop any attempt to fall back into old ways. Once progress is made the team will shift, from commitment over to confidence in their ability to achieve the goal, and they will no longer want to fall back into their old ways.

Communication is key at this point – keep people up to date with progress and highlight the little wins. If you don't set the tone, others will determine it for themselves.

High performance is so much fun; people are excited and cannot wait for the next meeting to see what is going to happen next! It's a fabulous place to be; you will feel extremely lucky, and things will begin to fall into your lap. This is the time to pat yourself on the back and say: 'Well done!' You created ambition with your team, and led the execution of the first initiatives which has got you to this place. Remember to keep communicating this success and remind people how far you have all come.

It's now about keeping up the momentum. This is the 'renewal' section of the model: ensuring that purpose, trust, DUMB goal and commitment remain solid, current and alive, which will keep your team in a high-performing state. The minute any of these qualities are no longer valid, teams will slip. Remember my earlier example; a high-performing team which achieved so much, but without a new goal, they quickly slipped from high performance.

Once people have experienced high performance, there will be a desire to stay there. In an organisation with the mindset and focus, high-performing teams become second nature, and DUMB goals part of the DNA. You will find leading these teams will be such a pleasure and exciting. The organisation will be naturally getting the best out of everyone. Passion, ambition and change will be the norm. This is rock'n'roll, baby! I am getting goosebumps just writing this, as I remember back to times I led teams like this. Have faith in the process, be brave and get started.

Can you imagine the difference between your organisation and your competitors once you have unleashed the power of teams!

Your teams are working with big ambition; people are working together for the greater good. There is a level of excitement, as people are making progress which they could not have imagined. They are learning new skills and being inspired every day to come to work and help make more progress. Compare this to an organisation where people come to work to collect a pay cheque, departments are working individually, and there is a culture of empire-building and patch protection, politics and hidden agendas. These teams are not excited to come to work – in fact they dread it! They have no ambition and are working to achieve their annual SMART goals. There are lots of meetings that achieve nothing. The comparison is night and day!

Now imagine you are a customer and the difference in the interactions with each company. Working with your company will be fun: your organisation will always be coming up with new, innovative solutions. Your people will always have a smile on their face and be excited about the future. Imagine the pay cheque company: people will be blaming others and other departments for issues. No one will be taking responsibility, and there is a sense they don't really care.

Which company would you want to work with – it's an easy decision, right?

Organisations need to be a fun place to work in, and people should be inspired. Can you see how a purpose-driven organisation with great teams achieves results? Your team will also think this company is the best place in which to work.

Some organisations that focus on being certified a 'great place to work' miss this crucial point. Normally it is something done by Human Resources: they focus on the brand of coffee in the staff canteen, or free lunches for their employees. This is all window dressing. Companies that are truly great places to work for are changing the world!

Get comfortable with ambiguity

There is one last challenge for the leaders managing high-performing teams: being comfortable with the unknown. High-performing teams will devise bold and ambitious strategies where the outcomes are difficult to accurately forecast. If the leadership pressures teams for sales upside, and then holds them accountable, teams will be driven to limit their ideas and ambitions. Instead, leaders need to understand and recognise the proposed outcomes of the strategies. Outcome scenarios can help the leaders and their teams to agree on the likely outcome. Once it's agreed, leadership and the team must move forward together – leadership in full support of the team. This support will drive the team to focus on execution and will also push teams further, as they will not want to let you down.

Create a leadership forum

By now you will be recognising the important role that team leaders play in high-performing teams – in fact, they are the most important ingredient. The leader that does not understand this will never create high-performing teams.

Building a leadership forum for leaders is essential. Before you embark on creating high-performing teams, you must educate them on their role as a leader. They must know the contents of this book, and understand the Drexler/Sibbet model and DUMB goals. They need to recognise the need for courage and confidence when establishing the team, in the early days before it has begun to see success.

Building a forum for these leaders will help you keep an eye on them, see the ones that are struggling and be able to support and coach them. It also allows them to express challenges they may be having, and get feedback from others who may be having similar issues too. Lastly, a forum gives your leaders something special: recognising the importance of their role. Make them feel special. By supporting them, they will lead teams to achieve high performance.

By now you may be feeling there is a lot to unpack in this chapter, and you might not know where to start. The best place is within your own leadership team. If you take the qualities of high-performing teams and the workshop and apply them to your team, the purpose being the company purpose, the rest remains the same. If you then do this with your own team, you will see and experience the benefit for yourself, which will help you identify these qualities you want in all your other teams, and find it so much easier to use the model with them.

With a small team which may be set up to work on something minor, it becomes easy to sit down at the first meeting and agree on a purpose: it's likely that you know each other already so trust is done; then you can agree the goal or outcome you are looking for, and decide how often you need to meet and confirm any resources you need. It can take less than 30 minutes. At least at this stage you are all aligned and focused on the outcome.

Team definition

Often in organisations today the word 'team' is used loosely for any group of people who meet together. Often these are not teams at all.

Defining what a team actually is will help you differentiate from 'groups' which may meet from time to time who currently label themselves as a team. As stated earlier, a team is 'a group of people *actively working together* to achieve a common goal'.

Not all groups that are currently called teams in your organisation need to be high-performing. Often, there are some meetings which are cross-functional and information-sharing: their purpose is to communicate between multiple departments. A distinction needs to be made between this type of meeting and a high-performing team meeting This distinction will help people recognise how to behave in meetings versus teams.

Over time, when your brand teams become high-performing teams, you will find less need for information-sharing meetings: department agendas will fade as people become more focused on achieving the goals of these teams, so make sure you understand the real purpose for meetings. High-performing teams are needed for groups who you are expecting to drive a strategy or outcome. Meetings to share information can remain as information-sharing meetings. The key is not to call these groups 'teams'. The distinction is important for people to understand expectations. Teams need purpose, trust, a goal and commitment. Information-sharing meetings just need an agenda.

Keep an eye on your teams, especially when first established: staying the course is all about supporting your teams and helping them through challenges which may come up. Once well established, it will become a lot easier as people will understand better how to make them successful. Remember that, at the beginning, everyone is learning – including your leaders. To close I will use a quote Kevin Roberts uses in his book *64 Shots* which highlights the opportunities and possibilities in your hands: 'One team, one dream, nothing is impossible.'[26]

Summary

1. The first few months after a team is established are crucial – the leader must keep the team

---

26 K Roberts, *64 Shots: Leadership in a Crazy World* (Powerhouse, 2016), p206

focused and aligned. While teams will be excited, they will not be confident that they can achieve the goal until some progress is made.

2. Team leaders must ensure that high-performing team qualities remain constant at all times.

3. Supporting and staying close to your team leaders is vital: they need support and courage to follow through.

4. Create a leadership forum to support and train your leaders to be their best.

5. Recognise the importance of identifying your high-performing teams and only calling these 'teams'. Forums for information-sharing are not teams. Historically, you may have called these 'teams'; now you should call them 'forums'. That way, people can distinguish the difference between better teams and forums.

9

The Power Of A Journey

Change is only hard when you are a victim of it. Lead the change, and it's fun!

If you speak with business leaders about a business journey, the topic almost always ends up in a discussion about change. Leaders talk about a challenging time when they had to change to save an organisation, but the majority are all about change when you are a victim rather than a leader of it.

Leading change successfully

The secret to leading change is to ensure your organisation is on a journey where change is forever constant but exciting: you are leading it, and your people want to see what will happen next. This understanding is crucial before considering key performance indicators (KPIs). Organisations that are on a journey will have KPIs that measure progress rather than binary achieved/not achieved goals.

While this may seem logical, many leaders don't discuss progress in terms of a journey to achieving something. Thinking of your organisation in this way will ensure that the KPIs created reflect progress to achieving the organisation's purpose.

From now on, all team presentations should be about the progress being made towards the organisation's purpose and the DUMB goals set up by your teams. This also includes the financial outcomes that have been achieved, and your ambitions for the future.

Being on a journey naturally creates great qualities within an organisation. This means from the outset that people see you, as the leader, are serious about achieving the organisation's purpose. This also means that progress and change are built into the way people work: they expect it.

The problem with change management

How often do you hear consultants talk about change management and how hard it is: that people don't like change, change is difficult? In all my experience, when you are leading the change and driving it, people love it and it is totally easy. Change that is difficult is change that is imposed on you. By building a purpose-driven organisation focused on delivering unique innovative programmes, always moving forward and improving, you are the leaders of change, not the victims, of it.

Journey comes with a language: calling it a journey, discussing progress to achievement, charting the course, where thinking ahead becomes second nature. As mentioned previously, innovation happens naturally when you have an ambitious target: people will be innovative by default, otherwise they will never get close to the goal.

It's about cause and effect. Imagine your competitors: they have consultants working on change management and big innovation programmes to try to get people to be innovative. Imagine the time they are wasting on this versus your teams focusing on making progress toward ambitious goals.

The benefits of change

For retaining talent

Change stops people getting set in their ways and becoming complacent. Most organisations strive to become a great place to work, providing benefits for their talent. They also work hard to retain talent, as the cost of replacing people is high – not just in financial terms, but the downtime and risk when training new people. If organisations operate like this, their people will be in their roles for some time, with limited room for promotion. What happens is they become stale: often after five or so years they look to exit the organisation; perhaps even sooner, with the younger generations.

In an organisation leading change and truly working on a journey, people are less likely to become stuck in their ways and roles. Constant change is good for people and their professional development: it helps your team remain engaged, as they are always moving between roles and learning new things.

For your team

Change is growth. If you're not changing, you're not growing. This is powerful: people who are growing and learning new things never become set in their ways, as they never get the opportunity.

When people are learning new things that help them grow professionally, they will be inspired and work hard to continue that learning. It becomes natural for people to feel fulfilled in their roles, as they are making progress on a journey. There is a sense of accomplishment of which they can be proud.

Imagine how different this is to a company with a financial target and people just going about their business. They become bored, just doing what needs to be done. There you will find learning teams trying to encourage people to learn new skills, but the trainees are disinterested and disengaged as there is no connection between the learning and work success.

This is such a contrast with teams on a journey, developing their learning – self-starters, motivated and engaged. Which type of team would you prefer?

For your organisation

If you're not changing, you're being left behind. The market is always changing! The journey also means you are changing and likely faster than the market – which means you are leaving your competitors behind.

This is extremely powerful. Even if your competitors are trying to copy you, by the time they catch up with your current execution, you have already evolved and moved on. This makes their execution look outdated and out of touch. The minute your competitors are copying you, you know you're a leader – your competitors are doomed to fail and become irrelevant. People want to be working with organisations that are always evolving and exciting to be around.

Jason Jennings, one of my mentors, wrote a book on the importance of reinvention.[27] It's a great read about the need to constantly reinvent yourself. This book has great examples of companies that have constantly changed and evolved through time.

KODAK VERSUS FUJIFILM: EMBRACING CHANGE SUCCESSFULLY

If Kodak were on a journey, they would have never stopped development of the digital camera. Kodak was the first to invent it, but never developed that technology because it was making too much money selling film. Kodak lost both its way and its advantage over competitors.

Fujifilm shows the difference in approach. The company went digital and now its cameras include film simulations, utilising their experience in film and transitioning the application into the digital world.

Kodak put short-term profits ahead of future success, while Fujifilm embraced change and looked at how it could use its history to create unique products for the future.

Fuji camera users talk about how the kit makes them 'feel', and how they 'love' the film simulations for providing artistic flair which they cannot get from other cameras.

Fuji found its way to compete to be unique. Being on the journey is the difference between Fuji and Kodak

---

27 J Jennings, *The Reinventors: How Extraordinary Companies Pursue Radical Continuous Change* (Portfolio, 2012)

– and to think that in 1990, Kodak was the eighteenth largest company listed on the New York Stock Exchange. Now it is virtually worthless.

If Kodak had been purpose-driven and less profit-driven, it would have realised the importance of developing digital like Fuji did, and be a highly successful company today.

Summary

1. Set your organisation on a journey to achieve its purpose, and change becomes natural and part of everyday business.

2. All organisational communication should use the language of a journey, and discuss progress to achieving the purpose or DUMB goals.

3. Change ensures that your team does not become stuck in its ways. It keeps people open to new ideas.

4. A journey allows your teams to recognise progress as a sense of achievement, rather than just at the point of overall success.

5. A journey means your organisation is always moving forward and reinventing itself, keeping you ahead of competitors and the market.

10

Measuring Success

Having a purpose statement is fantastic, but before you launch this with your team, you need to consider a few things. To make the link from purpose to strategy and then action, the organisation needs to be set up and aligned.

With an organisation being on a journey, the measure for KPIs will be different to the traditional KPIs in most organisations. Traditional KPIs are designed to ensure that standards are met: the aim of a KPI is to remain in a predefined range. For example, a forecast KPI would have a goal of 95–105% accuracy. These KPIs are great, and organisations should have these.

Purpose KPIs are more difficult to set, as the goals are more subjective. This is why few organisations have goals like this. In a world of possibilities, we don't see these as too hard, so we forget them. We ask, 'How can we?' When we design purpose KPIs, we need to have a standard way of asking questions, and a way to measure responses. The results of these KPIs are not mathematical in nature, but more charting progress milestones from one place to another.

The first step is to consider the organisation's current status versus the purpose:

- What is the delta?

- What initiatives are you going to introduce to help move your organisation closer to the purpose?

For example:

- Will you be working on trust with your team?

- Are you wanting to build better trust with your customers?

If so, you could create internal and external trust KPIs. Internal trust will not be how much your teams trust the organisation, but how much they trust each other – both could be measured in surveys. You might believe the key is alignment to customer issues ('self-orientation' in the Trust Equation): this would be something great to measure and chart progress in improving self-orientation.

Communicating KPIs

This is almost more important than the KPIs themselves. We need to recognise that how we measure something can impact how people act or behave and ensure that we don't create a KPI that pressures people to act in a certain way. This will only end with people manipulating outcomes to drive results. You want the results to be a natural measure; no one should have Human Resources goals around improving results.

It's amazing how often you see this in organisations, people pressured to get results. I'm sure you have purchased something and the person selling it to you will say:

> 'After the sale you will receive a survey of my performance/service, and I hope you can give me a ten out of ten! I will be penalised if I get anything less than an eight.'

You immediately feel sorry for them, so when the survey arrives you give them a ten, rather than your actual thoughts on the experience. They want numbers they can add up rather than insights which would help them improve. These KPIs are worthless:

the results don't help an organisation to understand in any way how they could improve.

With purpose progress KPIs that are not manipulated, the results are of value. Even if the results drop, it's good to know this rather than have people try to manipulate the results to hide true performance.

In a world of possibilities, we say:

- How interesting?
- What happened here?
- What is driving this?

This isn't a witch-hunt to fire the people responsible. In a purpose-driven culture or any organisation, people always want to do a good job: they work hard to achieve what they think their bosses want, and what they are being measured against. With this in mind, you can see how going on a witch-hunt is ridiculous. If things have gone wrong, recognise it: it's unlikely to have been anyone's deliberate intention to get bad results – so what happened? It is more likely to be circumstances out of their control. Talking to people and understanding what they believe to be the issues helps organisations to quickly take corrective action.

This approach will be refreshing for people: when they understand that bad news or mistakes are opportunities to learn and progress, they are more likely to be proactive at finding issues and recommending corrective action before these become bigger problems. The winning combination is when people feel empowered and inspired by this approach, aligned to the purpose of the organisation. When they see progress on the journey to the purpose collectively as a team, it provides a sense of accomplishment and pride in what they do.

Now KPIs are working for, not against, you!

Identify necessary changes

Before you launch your purpose statement and KPIs, are there any strategies or activities that need to be changed? It would be great to have something you can change immediately, to show your resolve to live the purpose.

For example, you may have a customer type which does not fit your new profile – perhaps they take up too much time and resources and don't align to your company's values. You might decide to reduce focus on these customers, with the aim of them moving on to a competitor. A lot of people will be scared to make this move, but there are always some customers who are not worth the effort – what is forgotten is the lost opportunity cost of keeping them. While your team is satisfying these customers, they are not free to find more of the right ones.

If you launch your purpose without discussing this with your team first, they will see it as just words on a page. There is, and should be, intent behind it – discuss and inform your team first, so they understand.

Next, consider your current financial KPIs in place, and how these could be changed to incorporate your purpose. For example, if teams regularly measure return on investment, you need to consider how you measure the return related to purpose rather than just the financial impact, and to make changes and decisions on that basis. While financial responsibility is important, often there will be times when an investment has no real tangible return except for benefiting the organisation's profile or improving a relationship with a key stakeholder.

Your success comes from a combination of everything your company does. This is why return-on-investment calculations can drive poor decision making. Look at your financial KPIs and consider adding some non-financial KPIs which align or link to your purpose. Again, this will show your teams that alignment to the purpose matters.

Some of the best investments I have made while in pharma have driven significant long-term performance, but it would be impossible to break down every initiative and attribute returns to the individual activities that drove this.

For example, with 'An Unstoppable Drive to Restore People's Lives', we measured our patient impact: how many patients entered our programmes, and how many were actively involved in the online community.

While we didn't want to create a perverse incentive, we used these as a measure of success as well as a monitor to understand how initiatives were resonating with stakeholders and patients. I didn't create incentives around a target, as this potentially would drive people to reach the target without understanding what was going on.

The focus would be on the target, instead of the initiatives to drive the target.

Underperformance should spark interest to understand why. The 'why' will help you understand the problem, while identifying it will help you set about making the improvements that drive better performance. Understanding the cause and effect of incentives is critical in a purpose-driven organisation. For example, if people are measured purely on financial KPIs, you are effectively saying to them, 'I will pay you if you make this margin.' In this case, you have given them permission to ignore the purpose.

You want your whole organisation to be working and aligned to achieving its DUMB goals, which links back to the purpose; but you can still have financial KPIs as a component. Also, importantly, everyone in the organisation should be incentivised on the same metrics.

In most of the companies I have worked, senior leaders had one incentive target: share price. Currently, we are seeing the effects of this, with most companies in the USA buying back their own shares to boost the price. This is money not being spent on research and development to futureproof organisations.

CEOs have large incentives tied to their organisation's share prices, similar to a senior executive's annual salary. This pressure – and the opportunity for such a large bonus – drives CEOs to think only about share price, rather than the organisation's long-term goals.

This has led (and driven) exponentially increased levels of borrowing money cheaply from banks to buy shares back, which in turn reduces their supply and drives up their price – and thereby CEO bonuses.

Launching the purpose

Once you have considered your KPIs and any strategies you need to change, you are ready to launch the purpose with your team. Can you imagine the difference between working in an organisation on a journey, with measures that everyone is working together on to achieve, versus an organisation with a purpose statement which has no connection to anything?

Can you imagine the difference in your teams' motivation levels, and how they will interact with customers? Your team is working as one, versus in an organisation where people are likely to be loyal to their division.

Measuring team performance

If you think back in the past to people in the team who were poor performers, in many cases it may not have been their performance to KPIs at fault; rather, their behaviour or attitude that led to this being the case. It's funny that people say they need ways to measure individuals, yet when they are in place, it is rare that this is the reason someone is found to be a poor performer.

This does not mean you should not challenge poor performance; in fact, if you want a high-performing team, it's essential for you to deal with this. If you consider poor performance and the Trust Equation, it is likely to be 'reliability', 'intimacy' or 'self-orientation' on which a poor performer will be scoring badly. If trust in the team is challenged, what do people do? They revert to acting as individuals and questioning why they are here.

If you don't deal with poor performers, your high performers will feel neglected. They are working hard, yet are treated the same as a poor performer. They may start thinking 'What is the point' and put in less effort. Failing to address poor performance brings everyone's performance down: it's more important to manage the poor performers than to recognise the good or high performers.

The ability to have crucial conversations is the key to tackling this: anyone who manages people needs to be trained in this area. If your people leaders are comfortable having these conversations, they won't think twice about speaking to the person who needs to improve early on. They will have the skill set to understand how to structure a conversation in a way that gets the message across regarding their performance in a positive – or at least not in a majorly negative – way.

High-performing teams have the conversations they need to have, and fast. The longer you leave it, the worse the problem will become and the more difficult the conversation will be. This means sorting things out quickly: acting immediately means the situation never reaches the stage where your high performers become annoyed at a colleague's lack of performance, or their impact on the team.

In most organisations, Human Resources expects a bell curve when it comes to rating your talent. If you are a leader that deals with poor performers, the bell curve is not a good way to measure your talent: in fact, it suggests that you should be happy with 50% of your people performing below average!

If you have a high-performing team and manage bad performance, the graph should look like this.

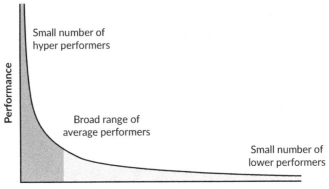

The Power-Law Distribution 'long-tail' curve

Josh Bersin explains this well in a *Forbes* article.[28] Your team should consist of a small number of hyper-performers, a broader range of great performers and an extremely low number of lower performers.

The key to getting this graph in your organisation is crucial conversations. You need to ensure all your people leaders are happy and competent to manage poor performance.

Summary

1. KPIs should measure your progress in achieving the organisation's purpose.

2. Being on a journey, KPIs should measure progress, as opposed to binary achieved/not achieved goals.

3. Watch your communication and how you use KPIs. Be interested in results, both good and bad. Ensure that no pressure is driving unintended employee behaviour.

4. What you measure you manage, so only measure the important stuff.

---

28   J Bersin, 'The myth of the Bell Curve: Look for the hyper-performers', *Forbes*, 19 February 2014, www.forbes.com/sites/joshbersin/2014/02/19/the-myth-of-the-bell-curve-look-for-the-hyper-performers

5. Deal with poor performers as much as you focus on high performers.

6. Ensure all your people leaders are equipped to have crucial conversations.

Conclusion

Congratulations for reading the book and getting to here! I hope I have convinced you of the power of a purpose-driven culture, unleashed by the power of your teams. Organisations have become soulless; they tick the box on 'purpose' by having some words on a wall, then never consider it again.

Demonstration is the only way to provide commitment to a purpose. People no longer trust what you say – they trust what you do. As I've emphasised throughout this book, the link from purpose to strategy and then execution is key. Without this, purpose is merely lip-service. Having strategies connected to your purpose means that your execution is your purpose demonstrated by action.

THE PURPOSE CULTURE JOURNEY

MINDSET

POSSIBILITIES

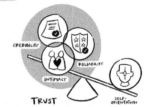

TRUST

PURPOSE

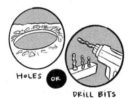

WHAT BUSINESS ARE YOU IN?

BUILD YOUR PURPOSE

TEAMS

DUMB GOALS

BUILDING TEAMS

UNLEASHING THE POWER OF TEAMS

SUSTAIN

THE POWER OF A JOURNEY

MEASURING SUCCESS

Purpose-driven organisations see the possibilities around them; people are coming up with exciting new ideas. Ideas are the currency of today. We stop hiring innovation consultants, and begin to see innovation naturally become part of our organisation's DNA.

You are no longer looking for your products to be your differentiator. Generic execution is boring for everyone – especially your customers; differentiating your execution based on purpose will inspire everyone from your team to your customers, setting you apart from your competitors.

DUMB goals for your teams are the fuel for ideas. They align everyone to the ambitious goal which initially no one has any idea how to achieve! Given time, and with leaders who keep teams focused, ideas and initiatives begin to take shape. Excitement starts to build, meetings become action-packed, workshop and brainstorming become the norm.

Picture your organisation right now. How much does it focus on internal versus external?

• Are your teams clear about what customers are really buying?

• Are they tailoring offerings to align to customers' needs?

- How much is compliance a blocker versus an enabler?

Right now, how excited are you about going to work tomorrow?

- What activities will be filling your day?
- Are the activities just time wasters?
- Are they helping the organisation on a journey to achieving something?

Without a journey we are not progressing. The time is now; seize the day. Take the reins of your organisation and lead it into a new future – a future with purpose, achieving a dream, not just a number!

Right now, you may be feeling anxious and not know where to start. Remember to refer to the Purpose Culture Journey illustration and use the following steps as a guide.

Step 1: Plan

Begin putting a plan in place to get your senior leaders' mindsets right. Bring possibilities to your leaders. Begin to teach them about the importance of trust, and how with this foundation you can transform relationships – both inside your organisation and, importantly, with your external stakeholders.

Step 2: Collaborate

Look for an external partner to help you: a person you trust, whose judgement you have faith in. It needs to be someone who can facilitate workshops for you: you cannot both facilitate and participate in workshops and hope to do so successfully.

Once you have this person in place, start with your leadership team. Use the high-performing teams' programme to build your organisation's purpose. Remember, if you think your leaders are not close enough to the business, get them to go out for a couple of days to do this – this is a vital step, as you need your team grounded in reality. It is easy to get disconnected in senior roles, and getting feedback from a team is not the same as seeing it for yourself first-hand.

Recognise that your senior leaders and most people in the organisation will be wanting to tell you what you want to hear. This is often the case, so get them out of the office.

Step 3: Workshop

Once all are grounded, organise a workshop to build your organisation's purpose. Consider taking your senior leadership team through the high-performing teams' programme.

Once you have got this far, congratulate yourself – you are halfway there! You should feel excited about the possibilities ahead of you. Your senior leaders should also be excited and wanting to share the purpose with their teams.

Remember to consider the launch: people will want to see action, not words. Are there changes you could implement immediately to help show your resolve to live the purpose?

Step 4: Audit

Next, do an audit of teams versus information-sharing meetings. Create your leadership forum for your team leaders and new ways of working.

Use your facilitator to help you train your leaders, so they are equipped to lead high-performing teams. Then they can cascade the workshop training with their teams.

Stay close to your leaders and monitor their progress: be there for them when they have questions and support them, as they are going through a huge learning phase.

Then, enjoy watching the transformation of your teams and the ambition of your organisation change.

See them become focused on achieving the big DUMB goal. The atmosphere in your office will become electric. People will be genuinely excited to come to work again, and believe they are making a difference.

Step 5: Compliance

Stay close to and work with your legal and compliance teams: help them understand their role in navigating teams through the process of implementing new and exciting strategies. Congratulate them when they find new ways to navigate the rules or grey areas, conforming while staying focused on the intention of the initiative. No longer will it just be about making money; it's about achieving the organisation's purpose for the benefit of your customers.

Then, congratulate yourself on leading a purpose-driven culture! You and your team will have a positive impact on the world, make a difference, destroy the competition and become more financially successful than you ever imagined. This means you can afford to pay your teams well, and support the community in ways not possible twelve months ago.

If you have any challenges, questions or feedback, I would love to hear your story. My contact details can be found at the back of the book.

Appendix: Build A Team Workshop

I have run many high-performing team workshops over the years and perfected a workshop structure for building teams. The process takes one-and-a-half days, in which time a team will build a team purpose, establish trust, create a DUMB goal and consider the time and resources necessary to build commitment.

For the workshop you will need flips charts, coloured markers and I would suggest having music available to use as people arrive at the workshop, in the breaks and also softly while people are working on activities. For the majority of the workshop I try to limit the use of PowerPoint slides and instead use flip charts, keeping the meeting interactive. Having music and using flip charts creates a fun and creative atmosphere.

I start with trust: I have found it makes sense to build and establish this before a team works together to create its purpose. I know this is different in the model. The model puts purpose first, as this determines who should be on the team when you are establishing a completely new one. In most cases, we are working with established teams, so it makes sense to begin with trust.

Step 1: Trust building

Activity 1: Break the ice

Building the bond of trust at the beginning makes the rest of the workshop better. To build trust people need to learn and understand each other so there is a connection beyond work.

Ask everyone to create a flip chart with four quadrants. In each quadrant they can draw or write:

1. Who I am at home

2. What I love about my job

3. Where I grew up

4. What my hobbies are

Next, ask people to present their flip charts to the rest of the team, and allow them to ask questions.

Remember also to complete the exercise yourself. While this is a simple exercise, it's a great way to find out about people, understand more about their up-bringing and who they are.

Activity 2: Colour exercise

Prior to the workshop, ask the team members to complete a colours personality assessment and bring this along. These can be found on the internet – the paid versions are recommended, as the quality of the assessment and report is better. I have used 'Insights Colours' and 'True Colours' in the past.

This exercise is good, as it helps people realise that everyone is different and we all have different strengths. The power of a team is having everyone play to their strengths. Set up the four corners of the meeting room with one of the colours, then ask people to move to the corner of the room representing their dominant colour.

In most cases this causes laughter and people pointing at each other, as they realise everyone's colours. Ask each colour group to write down what they love and what drives them crazy, then ask each group to present their colour. This is a lot of fun: it helps people play with extremes, highlighting how different each colour is.

It's important to recognise as the leader that it's good to have a balance of all colours on your team. There are no good or bad colours – they all bring value.

In this colours exercise, people begin to realise why they have had difficulty working with someone: it's likely they are opposites. Empathy and understanding mean that these people can work together better in the future. Also, it's useful for the leader to understand the people in their team.

After completing these exercises there will be a good atmosphere in the room and people will have laughed and got to know each other better.

Step 2: Purpose

This may feel repetitive, having a team purpose as well as the organisation's. The purpose here should just narrow down the organisation's purpose:

• What is the focus of this team?

• What is their part?

The reason for this is it aligns everyone to why they come to every meeting; without this, if you were to ask everyone the purpose of the team, they would all have a different answer. This purpose in the spirit of possibilities should be aspirational and positive in nature. When your team is asked by others, 'What is this team about?', they should be proud to tell them its purpose.

For this activity, print out lots of pictures of different things: for example, an eco-house, Steve Jobs, a rowing team, Virgin's rocket. Scatter them on the floor and ask people to pick up one of the pictures that reflects a quality you want in this team. Next, ask the team to present back, as the facilitator writes down the keywords and sense of what people said. Together with the team, then compose a purpose statement, taking into account their ideas and the organisation's purpose.

Remember: from the Drexler/Sibbet model the purpose is aspirational.

Step 3: DUMB goal

This is where the magic happens! By now the team should be excited: they have got to know everyone in the team, and are all aligned on the team purpose. The team is now ready to think about its DUMB goal.

DUMB goals are all about the dream, so obviously we start with talking about that.

D - Dream-driven

Start this process by getting people to think about their rocking-chair moment for this team. We want people to imagine they are telling a young child about this team they were on, and what it achieved, but keeping in mind the time frame for our goal should be two to three years.

In some cases, perhaps with a new product, it is going to be about launch, so include some of the qualities that would see this launch be one of the most successful. Describe it in detail:

• What will it look like?

• How is the team feeling?

• What will we need to do to accomplish the goal?

• What will customers be saying about us?

You will begin to see people's eyes light up about the possibilities ahead.

Next, get people to share their dreams with the team. Have your facilitator take notes on the flip chart, and work as a team to create one goal from it.

Depending on the size of the group, break them into two groups of around five people. Get them to take a flip chart each and create a *Time* magazine cover for what people will be saying about you when you have achieved the goal: include a headline, subtitle and picture:

- What will be the picture?
- What will be the inserts around the picture?
- What will stakeholders be saying?
- What will be happening with our competitors?

This exercise is great at getting people to imagine not the goal, but its outcome. This is extremely important, as it begins to let us understand what needs to happen to make the goal a reality.

Once the groups have done this, share back and agree together on what people like from each, then create one cover. After the workshop, produce and frame it for the office. It becomes a great reminder for the team what they are aiming for, and what they are wanting to achieve.

U – Uplifting

Now the team has in their imagination what amazing success looks like, check the goal with them again. Make sure from the *Time* magazine exercise that people don't want to adjust any of the working.

Obviously now you live in a world of possibilities, it goes without saying that you would do this in an uplifting way. Make sure the goal has an external focus, as your success will come from external factors. Any internal challenges are within our control, so there should be an expectation that these issues will be solved. The goal should also align with the ambitions of your customers, as this ensures your teams remain customer-focused.

I have seen great examples of teams' planning to achieve a successful launch, but more details about the degree of success, what customers will be saying are required. They need to know how this product will change the landscape. Make sure the goal is deeper than just 'being successful'.

M – Method

This is the most important step of the process: how you make sure the dream becomes a reality. It's time to begin thinking about the how, but don't panic – you and the team don't have the answers yet.

For this step, consider who are the key stakeholders needed to achieve the goal's success. List the stakeholders down the left-hand side of a flip chart, with two columns to the right. In the first column, write the current position of this stakeholder now. Do this for each stakeholder.

In the second column, what would they need to think for you to achieve the goal? What would their future position need to be? Remember the example from Chapter 6:

Current position	Delta	Future state
Purely price-focused	The methods need to bridge the gap from current to future	Recognised value beyond price

You now know the delta between the current position and the future state. It is important for everyone in the team to understand the gap. This can seem like a massive gap, but people shouldn't immediately try to solve it or worse, dismiss the idea that it can be achieved. At this point, it's fine just for them to recognise the gap.

Having lived in the world of SMART goals, people have been programmed to make sure that goals are measurable and realistic. Instead, we're asking them here to think the complete opposite – and for some, this will be difficult. As the leader, it's important for you to explain this to the team: from now on, their purpose when in team meetings is to begin to figure out the how.

In the SMART world, people feel they have to solve everything immediately, otherwise they have failed.

In a world of DUMB goals, we want people to understand the gap, be comfortable with it. To go away and start thinking about ideas or things to try to close the gap. You also want to encourage your team to talk about the goal with stakeholders, ask them what they think. Often, people will want to help, as your goal is exciting and for the good of your customers.

One of the key ingredients people always forget is the power of time: our brains have an amazing propensity to percolate ideas, given the time to do so. We have all had moments in the shower or times when talking with someone and an idea pops into our head. We need to make sure people don't feel pressured to find solutions straightaway. We want them to be inquisitive. By definition, big goals can never be solved immediately, otherwise they wouldn't be so.

The power of these methods is about having everyone in our teams focused and considering about what we can try to progress people's thinking closer to our goal.

B - Behaviours

Behaviours are another key to success: it's the team leader who has to stay focused on this. If the leader slips back from possibilities, everyone else will as well, so it's crucial to set an example. If you are an existing team, this is even more important. In the absence of

162

having big goals historically, meetings will have been full of day-to-day things which could have been handled in an email: mostly information-sharing.

Now we have a DUMB goal, we need meetings to zero in on the how, and the learning for what has just taken place. For example, news may have come out about one of your stakeholders, or something about your competitors may have changed. You may have had a meeting with a stakeholder and received some new information. Consider any new information as good, regardless of whether you think it helps or sets you back. Information is progress, which helps you continue to build the path to success. Bad news doesn't mean you give up: it simply means learning from it, and thinking about how it changes your future plans. As the team leader, be sure to stop people when they try to fill meetings with the day-to-day.

The first meeting after this workshop is the most important: it sets the tone for all meetings from here onwards. To help people with this transition, try to hold the meeting in a different place to where you regularly meet. Make sure the agenda is aligned to the DUMB goal, and look to workshop people's initial ideas. Come up with a plan for the next couple of months of things you need to do to uncover the how: this will help the team stay on track.

I cannot stress enough the leader's role in keeping the team concentrating on the new goals and stopping people from falling back into their old ways. Initially, they won't understand that this is now the focus and getting the day-to-day complete is an expectation. There does not need to be a long conversation or presentation on what has been completed. Everyone should know the plan and be executing to it.

It's one of the characteristics of a leader that he not doubt for one moment the capacity of the people he's leading to realize whatever he's dreaming. Imagine if Martin Luther King had said, 'I have a dream. Of course, I'm not sure they'll be up to it.'
— Benjamin Zander[29]

This quote should help you stay on track: provide the team with confidence to follow through on the new ways, not to reset.

I know from experience if you do this, you will look back in the future and be astonished and proud of what your team has achieved.

Enjoy leading a high-performing team. Heading up a team like this is the best part of being a leader; you will be amazed at what you achieve.

---

29 B Zander, *The transformative power of classical music* [TED talk], 2008, www.ted.com/talks/benjamin_zander_the_transformative_power_of_classical_music

The last thing to do before ending the workshop is to decide together how often you should meet, and for how long.

Then, to close the workshop, take a photo of everyone together with the team purpose and DUMB goal. A picture you will use to tell the story from the beginning.

Acknowledgements

Throughout my career, Jason Jennings' books have been an inspiration to me and have always given me confidence to follow through with what I believed. The conference where I met Jason for the first time set me on a path which I will always be proud of, and grateful for.

Sadly, before this book was published, Jason passed away. He did read the draft and was writing the foreword for the book. I will miss him.

I would like to acknowledge the teams I have led over the years, especially my New Zealand pharma team that achieved so much at the same time as growing together, and having fun. I love your work.

The Author

Nick Leach is a passionate leader based in Sydney. With twenty years' experience in Australia, New Zealand, Asia, Japan and China, his company, On-Purpose Solutions, works with businesses to achieve outstanding results.

Leading multiple teams, Nick has defied logic to achieve what others thought impossible. He coaches business leaders and has developed successful programmes based on personal experience.

www.on-purpose.solutions
nick@on-purpose.solutions

Made in the USA
Las Vegas, NV
28 May 2023

72658135R00098